Tenuous Threads & *One of the Lucky On*

THE AZRIELI SERIES OF HOLOCAUST SURVIVOR MEMOIRS: PUBLISHED TITLES

ENGLISH TITLES

Album of My Life by Ann Szedlecki
Bits and Pieces by Henia Reinhartz
A Drastic Turn of Destiny by Fred Mann
E/96: Fate Undecided by Paul-Henri Rips
Fleeing from the Hunter by Marian Domanski
From Generation to Generation by Agnes Tomasov
Gatehouse to Hell by Felix Opatowski
Getting Out Alive by Tommy Dick
If Home Is Not Here by Max Bornstein
Knocking on Every Door by Anka Voticky
Little Girl Lost by Betty Rich
Memories from the Abyss by William Tannenzapf / *But I Had a Happy Childhood*
  by Renate Krakauer
The Shadows Behind Me by Willie Sterner
Spring's End by John Freund
Survival Kit by Zuzana Sermer
Tenuous Threads by Judy Abrams / *One of the Lucky Ones*
  by Eva Felsenburg Marx
Under the Yellow and Red Stars by Alex Levin
The Violin by Rachel Shtibel / *A Child's Testimony* by Adam Shtibel

TITRES FRANÇAIS

L'Album de ma vie par Ann Szedlecki
Cachée par Marguerite Elias Quddus
Étoile jaune, étoile rouge par Alex Levin
La Fin du printemps par John Freund
Fragments de ma vie par Henia Reinhartz
Frapper à toutes les portes par Anka Voticky
De génération en génération par Agnes Tomasov
Matricule E/96 par Paul-Henri Rips
Objectif : survivre par Tommy Dick
Souvenirs de l'abîme par William Tannenzapf / *Le Bonheur de l'innocence*
  par Renate Krakauer
Un terrible revers de fortune par Fred Mann
Traqué par Marian Domanski
Le Violon par Rachel Shtibel / *Témoignage d'un enfant* par Adam Shtibel

Tenuous Threads
Judy Abrams

One of the Lucky Ones
Eva Felsenburg Marx

SECOND PRINTING

Copyright © 2012 The Azrieli Foundation and others

THE AZRIELI FOUNDATION
www.azrielifoundation.org

Cover and book design by Mark Goldstein
Endpaper maps by Martin Gilbert
Inside maps by François Blanc
Family trees by Keaton Taylor

LIBRARY AND ARCHIVES CANADA CATALOGUING IN PUBLICATION

Abrams, Judy, 1937–
    Tenuous threads/ Judy Abrams. One of the lucky
ones/ Eva Felsenburg Marx.

(Azrieli series of Holocaust survivor memoirs. Series IV)
Includes bibliographical references and index.
ISBN 978-1-897470-28-2

1. Abrams, Judy, 1937–. 2. Marx, Eva Felsenburg, 1937–. 3. Holocaust, Jewish (1939–1945) – Hungary – Personal narratives. 4. Holocaust, Jewish (1939–1945) – Slovakia – Personal narratives. 5. Jewish children in the Holocaust – Hungary – Biography. 6. Jewish children in the Holocaust – Slovakia – Biography. 7. Hidden children (Holocaust) – Hungary – Biography. 8. Hidden children (Holocaust) – Slovakia – Biography. 9. Holocaust survivors – Canada – Biography. I. Azrieli Foundation II Marx, Eva Felsenburg, 1937–. One of the lucky ones III. Title. IV Series: Azrieli series of Holocaust survivor memoirs. Series IV

D804.48.A27 2011   940.53′18083   C2011-904089-1

PRINTED IN CANADA

The Azrieli Series of Holocaust Survivor Memoirs

Contents

Series Preface   ix

About the Glossary   xi

Introduction *by Mia Spiro*   xiii

TENUOUS THREADS

Map   1

Chestnut Boulevard   7

The Saving Beads   13

My First and Only Christmas   19

The Saving Cry   25

Afterward   31

Dragons and Departures   39

Escape   47

New Adjustments   55

Dead Man's Suit   63

My Mother's Secrets   69

ONE OF THE LUCKY ONES

Map   77

Brno   83

My First Escape   91

In Hiding   101

After the War   107
Leaving Europe   117
Life's Journey   125
Epilogue   133

Glossary   137
Photographs   151
Index   177

Series Preface:
In their own words...

In telling these stories, the writers have liberated themselves. For so many years we did not speak about it, even when we became free people living in a free society. Now, when at last we are writing about what happened to us in this dark period of history, knowing that our stories will be read and live on, it is possible for us to feel truly free. These unique historical documents put a face on what was lost, and allow readers to grasp the enormity of what happened to six million Jews – one story at a time.

David J. Azrieli, C.M., C.Q., M.Arch
Holocaust survivor and founder, The Azrieli Foundation

Since the end of World War II, over 30,000 Jewish Holocaust survivors have immigrated to Canada. Who they are, where they came from, what they experienced and how they built new lives for themselves and their families are important parts of our Canadian heritage. The Azrieli Foundation's Holocaust Survivor Memoirs Program was established to preserve and share the memoirs written by those who survived the twentieth-century Nazi genocide of the Jews of Europe and later made their way to Canada. The program is guided by the conviction that each survivor of the Holocaust has a remarkable story to tell, and that such stories play an important role in education about tolerance and diversity.

Millions of individual stories are lost to us forever. By preserving the stories written by survivors and making them widely available to a broad audience, the Azrieli Foundation's Holocaust Survivor Memoirs Program seeks to sustain the memory of all those who perished at the hands of hatred, abetted by indifference and apathy. The personal accounts of those who survived against all odds are as different as the people who wrote them, but all demonstrate the courage, strength, wit and luck that it took to prevail and survive in such terrible adversity. The memoirs are also moving tributes to people – strangers and friends – who risked their lives to help others, and who, through acts of kindness and decency in the darkest of moments, frequently helped the persecuted maintain faith in humanity and courage to endure. These accounts offer inspiration to all, as does the survivors' desire to share their experiences so that new generations can learn from them.

The Holocaust Survivor Memoirs Program collects, archives and publishes these distinctive records and the print editions are available free of charge to libraries, educational institutions and Holocaust-education programs across Canada, and at Azrieli Foundation educational events. They are also available for sale to the general public at bookstores. All editions of the books are available for free download on our web site at: www.azrielifoundation.org.

The Azrieli Foundation would like to express appreciation to the following people for their invaluable efforts in producing this series: Simone Abrahamson, Florence Buathier, Darrel Dickson (Maracle Press), Sir Martin Gilbert, Stan Greenspan, Arnaud Regnauld, Sylwia Szymańska-Smolkin, Keaton Taylor, Robert Jan van Pelt, Lise Viens, Margie Wolfe and Emma Rodgers of Second Story Press, and Piotr Wróbel.

About the Glossary

The memoirs in this volume contain a number of terms, concepts and historical references that may be unfamiliar to the reader. For information on major organizations; significant historical events and people; geographical locations; religious and cultural terms; and foreign-language words and expressions that will help give context and background to the events described in the text, please see the glossary beginning on page 137.

Introduction

On a sunny spring day in 1944 in Vráble, a small town in the southern region of Slovakia, six-year-old Eva Felsenburg is disguised in peasant clothes by her grandmother and sent on an unusual trip. Her grandparents have hired a man to take her by bicycle to meet her father under a bridge in the nearby town of Nitra to go into hiding. She feels her grandmother's tears on her cheek as she holds her tight to say goodbye. Eva wonders why she is being sent away. Only one hundred kilometres away in Budapest, Hungary, another seven-year-old little girl by the name of Judit Grünfeld is led by her mother down a tree-lined avenue to the gates of a convent. Her parents have told her that from now on she is no longer Judit, a Jewish girl, but Ilona Papp, a devout Catholic child. Judit feels queasy as her mother turns to leave her with a black-clad nun. She has always been good at make-believe, but this time the game is for real.

Now grandmothers of children the very same age, Eva Felsenburg Marx and Judy Grünfeld Abrams share their stories with us. Each narrative weaves richly depicted images and moments of an inexplicable time in history when young Jewish children were hunted down and the only way to survive was to become invisible. At the start of World War II, there were approximately 1.6 million Jewish children living in occupied Europe. By May 1945, less than 7 per cent of them had survived. Historians estimate that more than one million, and perhaps as many as 1.5 million children were killed by the Nazis over the course of the war. "I was one of the lucky ones," writes Eva at the opening of her memoir. Indeed she was. An estimated six million Jews were murdered during the Holocaust at the hands of the Nazis, but, as special targets for annihilation, children had a far lower survival rate than adults. Of the children who did survive, most were hidden – sometimes with their parents, but most often without. They were given false identities, hidden in convents, squirrelled away in the apartments of friends or adopted by Christian families; occasionally, they even ended up wandering alone, left to fend for themselves. Yet, even for those children who did manage to escape death, survival meant a rupture in their otherwise normal childhoods and an inheritance of insecurity and fear. Exiled from worlds that ceased to exist and encumbered by the suffering of their parents, the legacy of being "lucky" can often be a burden. For these formerly hidden children, the war and its aftermath can be a painful recollection.

Although they never met, the parallels between Eva and Judy's experiences as child survivors of the Holocaust are striking. In their narratives, past and present meld together as they struggle to remember and understand the psychological impact of the Holocaust and the complicated inheritance of their escape. As Jewish children in occupied Europe in the early 1940s, they had to be watchful, observant, and often rely on their precociousness and model behaviour to adapt to new situations both during and after the war. Memoirs that highlight young children's viewpoints of the Holocaust – like these two accounts – are both rare and indispensable from a historical and narrative perspective. They vividly unlock the past, allowing us glimpses into the mysteries of childhood: the taste of freshly baked bread, the smell of chestnut blossoms, the feel of a grandmother's touch, the sound of laughter, the fickleness of childhood friendships, the cool splash of water on a warm summer's day, the delight in a new coat. At the same time, by inhabiting the naive world of the child, we too enter their universe of incomprehensibility, knowing full well the imminent danger that lurks in the gaps between what the child can and cannot know: relatives who disappear, parents who are sent to concentration camps, homes that are destroyed by bombs. In this sense we are made cognizant of the precarious, and somewhat arbitrary circumstances that keep these children safe.

Of course, the paradox for children growing up during the Holocaust is that they were seldom fully aware of the peril they faced as Jews. Unlike their parents, they lacked the perspective to compare their own reality with a pre-war past and there was a limit to what their young minds could absorb. Both Judy and Eva were not even born when Hitler and the Nazi party rose to power in 1933 and two years later, in September 1935, passed the anti-Jewish edicts that became known as the Nuremberg Laws. From that point on, Jews in Germany were officially defined by heredity rather than religion, and, as "non-Aryans," were stripped of their citizenship and other fundamental rights. What made Jewish children particular targets is that they came to be seen as "the seed of the subhuman" that threatened to pollute the Aryan race. Judy and Eva were only toddlers when Nazi troops first occupied Czechoslovakia to establish the Protectorate of Bohemia and Moravia and the semi-autonomous Republic of Slovakia in March 1939 and then invaded Poland in September 1939, launching World War II. The Nazis soon put into place the same anti-Jewish laws in the lands they occupied. The only world Judy and Eva knew as children was a world at war. But even if they had been able to understand the impact of these political events, the gravity of the Nazi menace would have been impossible for them to comprehend. It was difficult enough to absorb the fact that a regime would want to target Jews for murder – but children? How can we fathom a genocide that targeted this most vulnerable and powerless segment of society?

The psychological challenges children had to face and the coping skills they had to develop to withstand the fear, loneliness, silence, separation and shame resulting from hiding their identities are essential to understanding the impact of the Nazi period. Games of make-believe became essential tools for children like Judy and Eva, who as youngsters became masters of disguise and connoisseurs of pretending. Remembering her life at age seven with the Ursuline nuns in the Hungarian countryside, Judy recalls that she was so good at pretending to be a Christian "that I had made my previous, Jewish self fade, receding into forbidden recesses of my mind." Eva was only two years old when she boarded the train to Vráble with her loving maid, Marka, in March 1939: "[I] have a vague memory of that journey. If the Germans, who interrogated everyone, asked about our identities, I was to say that Marka was my mother." This type of mentally and emotionally complex role-playing became typical for Jewish children who had to learn quickly to fit into every situation and avoid suspicion. In one agonizing moment in Judy's story she recalls her first day at the convent as she struggles to adapt. "I hated the 'skin' of hot milk. Was this unchristian? I closed my eyes and, almost choking on the slimy film, gulped down the warm liquid without pausing for breath."

As these stories reveal, despite the impression that hidden children were "innocently secure," the uneasy sense that they were endangered most certainly had an impact. There are times when both Eva and Judy are clearly aware that they are on the verge of being caught and that being caught is a deadly prospect. Judy, for instance, relates the terror and dread she felt in a bomb shelter when a Hungarian fascist Arrow Cross officer arrived to hunt down hidden Jews and singled her out as "looking Jewish." Eva, too, recalls the time when their unreliable "rescuer" put her family in jeopardy by having a German soldier over for dinner, forcing them to huddle into the pantry and hide. "I remember how terrified we all were when I once sneezed, afraid that her German boyfriend would overhear. She would lord it over us, threatening to denounce us, demanding more and more money. 'Unless you pay more, I'll go to the SS!' she would shout." Considering that many hidden Jews were indeed exploited, blackmailed and then denounced to the authorities, these situations were terrifying.

As readers we feel distress for these young children who were stalked in the outside world, indebted to those who rescued them and saddled with the enormous responsibility of adjusting, often without the support of their parents. Separation from and reunification with parents was especially challenging for Jewish children during the war years. Common to the many stories of hidden children, the profound loss and trauma connected with parting remains beyond the reaches of memory and articulation. With typical vagueness, Judy writes of separating from her mother: "Surely my mother waved as she turned from the gate that closed behind me. We would not see each other again for more than a year. How did she say goodbye?" Reunification with parents after long stretches of time was conflicted as well. Eva describes seeing her father after a separation of five years with similar ambiguity: "I don't remember much about my reunion with my father under that bridge on the outskirts of Nitra. I was almost seven years old and hadn't seen my father in five years. I didn't even know what he looked like." Even seeing her beloved and cherished mother fills young Eva with anxiety: "What would I say to her? What would she be like?" Some child survivors like Judy felt shame at their unexpected reactions to their estranged mothers and fathers. "Could I be right?" the small girl wonders. "I looked at the small, thin, nervous lady, whom I would call Anyu (Mother) again and remembered another Anyu from before." These situations were never ideal for building a strong sense of security.

Memory itself is a recurring theme in these stories. For both Judy and Eva, the lasting impact of their experiences during the Holocaust reaches into the deep recesses of the mind, at times emerging as clear recollections, often as lingering impressions and sometimes as nightmares. We can only admire the resilience, optimism and dogged determination to live life with humour and compassion as each young woman confronts new challenges while adapting to life in Canada after the war. Despite witnessing the struggles of their war-damaged parents and having to make up for lost years of schooling, Eva and

Judy both excel academically, form bonds of friendship and lay the foundations for their own independent lives. Each individual story is a rare reflection and compelling testimony of resilience, healing and courage. But in reading these stories, we also must remember all those children who were silenced: the 1.5 million young souls who never had the chance to tell their own tales. Through stories like these we, too, lament these lost voices as we wonder at the truly unique experience for children in the Holocaust – surviving.

JUDY ABRAMS: TENUOUS THREADS

Born in Budapest, Hungary on April 28, 1937, to Renée (née Kaba) and László Grünfeld, Judy Abrams was the only child of middle-class parents. Her father's family were wine merchants who had moved to Budapest from northeastern Hungary. Her mother's ancestors, the Deutsch-Müller family, had lived in Budapest since the nineteenth century. At the time Judy was born, there was a large thriving Jewish population of 825,000 in Hungary. At the end of World War II, less than one-third of them had survived. More than 550,000 Hungarian Jews had been killed or died of starvation and disease in concentration camps, most in the very last year of the war. The remarkable brutality and speed in which they were delivered to their deaths so close to Germany's defeat was especially appalling.

Judy's family, like many Budapest Jews, had modernized and integrated into the larger Hungarian Christian populace and enjoyed a prosperous and cultured life. Judy went to a Montessori day school; she and her parents spoke Hungarian and German rather than Yiddish; they participated in Budapest cultural life; and many of their friends and colleagues were either not Jewish or had intermarried. Conversions to Christianity were also common – in 1941 when racial laws were introduced in Hungary, 100,000 Jews were registered as converts to Catholicism. Jews in Hungary had not always enjoyed the tolerance of the early twentieth century. Only in 1867 and 1895 did laws recognizing Judaism as a state religion, equal to Catholicism or Protestantism, give Jews equal citizenship rights, ushering in what is often referred to as the Golden Era of Hungarian Jewry (1867–1918). From the seventeenth to the mid-nineteenth century, as was true in many other European countries, Hungarian Jews were subjected to discriminatory laws that restricted where they could live, placed quotas on education, required them to pay extra taxes and otherwise limited their rights for economic and judicial equality. By the early 1900s, however, emancipated Jews rapidly began making significant contributions to science, art, literature, politics and sports. In the 1920s, Jews made up 6 per cent of the Hungarian population but constituted half the lawyers and doctors, 35 per cent of journalists and editors, and owned 40 per cent of all business firms.

What seemed like a tolerant, secure and protected future for Jews in Hungary nevertheless proved to be unstable. With the collapse of the Hapsburg Empire in World War I and the ensuing political crisis in Hungary, Jews became scapegoats for conservative nationalists and communist revolutionaries alike. Propaganda on the left characterized Jews as middle-class capitalists and enemies of the working class. Counter-revolutionary forces on the right targeted Jews as leftists and blamed them for the territorial losses during World War I, when Hungary lost two-thirds of its land to Czechoslovakia. The situation did not improve when a new Hungarian government was formed in 1920, proclaiming Admiral Miklós Horthy as regent and head of state. Jews in Hungary, who had enjoyed so much freedom during the Golden Era, were now one of the first minorities in Europe to be subject to anti-Jewish legislation, the *Numerous Clausus* Act (1920), which once again limited Jewish admission to institutions of higher learning. A decade later, in 1932, Hungary appointed a new, pro-fascist and ultra-nationalist conservative prime minster, Gyula Gömbös, who became one of the first foreign leaders to meet with Hitler and support the Nazi regime. Tens of thousands of Jewish men were drafted into the Hungarian army in forced labour battalions from 1941 to 1944 to support the Third Reich's campaign against the Soviet Union. Singled out with yellow armbands, they were subjected to dreadful treatment, given the most dangerous tasks and denied proper equipment and clothing. Close to 42,000 of these labour servicemen died along the Soviet front.

The Nazi plan to annihilate all the Jews of Europe, better known as the "Final Solution," was nevertheless late in reaching Hungary. The pro-Nazi Hungarian government had only adopted some of the Nazi anti-Jewish policies and, at the same time that Nazi Germany began its reign of terror against Jews in the occupied countries, Jewish leaders in Hungary remained optimistic about their fate. Their confidence may have been naive, but not difficult to imagine. They had heard rumours of deportations of Jews in Germany, Austria, Poland and Czechoslovakia, but had little idea that Jews were being murdered on a large scale in death camps. They were also convinced that Hungary's new prime minister, Miklós Kállay, who had been elected in 1942, would protect them. What changed the fate of Hungarian Jews was somewhat paradoxical. In 1943, Kállay began making secret overtures to Western powers to extract Hungary from the war and its alliance with Germany. When the Nazis uncovered Kállay's plan in October 1944, Hitler ordered the overthrow of the government. The ousted leader was sent to Dachau concentration camp in Germany and replaced by Ferenc Szálasi, a strong Nazi supporter and rabid antisemite who swiftly established an Arrow Cross Party dictatorship.

In March 1944, an arrangement to transport Jewish male workers to Poland to "help" the war effort turned into a design to deport all Hungarian Jews. On March 19, 1944, Germany occupied Hungary and steps to render Hungary *judenrein* (free of Jews) began in earnest. Adolf Eichmann, head of the Gestapo department charged with the implementation of the Final Solution, arrived with a special unit of two hundred commandos to begin isolating Jews, confiscating their property, putting them into ghettos and deporting them. On April 5, 1944, all Hungarian Jews were ordered to wear the yellow Star of

David in public. Deportations to the death camps began on May 15, 1944, with the help of the Arrow Cross brigades and the cooperation of the Hungarian civil services. Within the short span of two months, more than 437,685 Hungarian Jews were transported to Auschwitz, mostly from the countryside outside of Budapest. The majority of them were sent directly to the gas chambers.

Some individuals, like Judy's father, were wary of the changes happening in Hungary in 1944 and managed to arrange refuge for their children or families. Judy mentions that her father had heard accounts of the concentration camps from escaped inmates, most probably from the report circulated by Rudolf Vrba and Alfred Wetzler after the two men miraculously escaped Auschwitz on April 7, 1944, and fled to Slovakia. The Slovak Jewish Council passed the Vrba-Wetzler report on to Jewish leaders in Hungary to warn them. Many Jews, however, still refused to believe that the Nazis, with the aid of the Arrow Cross regime, intended to murder them.

Judy's father was not among them – he obtained false identity documents showing that Judy was an "Aryan" Catholic girl, Ilona Papp, and with the help of a loyal family friend, Mária Babar, Judy was placed in the custody of Ursuline nuns. Thousands of Jewish children like Judy were saved by the kindness of friends and Christian institutions that offered protection to Jews. Yet even these establishments were not safe from the SS and the Arrow Cross officers who conducted raids to find hidden Jews. Fearing for her safety, Mária took Judy back to Budapest after a few months to hide her in her own apartment. There, along with Judy's grandmother and Aunt Marika, all of whom were living under aliases, Judy was able to wait out the war. In 1994, Mária was honoured by Yad Vashem, The Holocaust Martyrs' and Heroes' Remembrance Authority, as one of the Righteous Among the Nations.

While Judy was at the convent in the countryside, plans for deporting the 247,000 Jews who were still left in Budapest in April 1944 were in full swing. On May 3, 1944, Jews were ordered to register their property and on June 16 they were forced to relocate to "yellow star houses" (sárga csillagos házak). Some Budapest Jews, like Judy's parents, ended up on trains to Bergen-Belsen in Germany to be used as "exchange Jews" – held for ransom at the concentration camp to be traded for money and industrial material, which by then the losing German army desperately needed. The Vrba-Wetzler report had by this time reached the wider world and the United States, the Vatican and neutral countries such as Switzerland and Sweden had finally become concerned. The Swedish government authorized humanitarian worker Raoul Wallenberg to distribute Swedish passports and set up "safe houses," saving thousands of Jews.

Why the rest of the Jews of Budapest were not deported remains a matter of some debate, but at the end of October 1944 the deportations suddenly came to a halt. Nonetheless, the Arrow Cross brigade continued to harass and beat Jews in the city. That December, when Judy, along with her grandmother and aunt were in hiding in Mária's apartment, was an especially devastating month. Tens of thousands of Jews like Judy and her relatives had tried to wait out the war by hiding in Christian homes. The Arrow Cross rounded up thousands of them, brought them to the banks of the Danube River and shot them. By the end of the war, when Soviet troops liberated the city on February 13, 1945, slightly more than 100,000 Jews were left in the city. Less than half of the pre-war Jewish population of 247,000 had managed to survive.

Judy was reunited with her parents after the war. For many Jewish families in Budapest, re-adjusting to post-war life was a painful and difficult process. Relatives and friends were confirmed dead or missing and the new Hungarian Communist Party in power considered merchants like the Grünfelds to be "class aliens." In the face of these realities, Judy's parents made plans to emigrate from Hungary to Canada. Although Canada had shamefully closed its door to Jewish refugees during the war years, immigration policies after the war had become somewhat more relaxed, and Judy's aunt in Canada was able to sponsor them. In 1948 Judy and her parents traded their apartment as a "fee" for Hungarian passports to leave the country and made their way to a displaced persons (DP) camp in the American-controlled section of Austria. From there they became part of nearly 40,000 Holocaust survivors who made their way to Canada in the late 1940s, many of whom settled in Montreal.

Judy's parents faced numerous challenges settling into their new lives in Montreal. Her father suffered both financial and health troubles, and her mother struggled to keep the family afloat. Still, Judy managed to excel in her studies at Montreal High School for Girls and West Hill High School, graduating with a History prize in 1954. She received a teaching certificate from MacDonald College in 1955 and graduated with a BA from Sir George Williams College (now Concordia University) in Montreal three years later. During this time she also met her future husband, Tevia Abrams, at university. They married in 1957 and had two children, Ira, born in 1964, and Eugene, born in 1965. Judy was much loved as an elementary school teacher and later as a French specialist, teaching for the Protestant School Board of Greater Montreal until 1968, when she and Tevia moved to Michigan with their two small children to enrol in graduate programs at Michigan State University. Tevia did his doctoral research in Indian folk theatre and communications, which took them to India for a year (later returning there to work from 1990 to 1993) and Judy earned a master's degree in linguistics. In 1972 the family moved to New York City, where Tevia worked at the United Nations Population Fund and Judy taught French and English as a second language until 2002 (she earned a second MA in Teaching English to Speakers of Other Languages [TESOL] in 1983). She now spends her time between her two homes in New York and Montreal, where her son Eugene and his wife, Julie, live and where her grandson Émile was born in 2001.

Parts of Judy Abrams' life story appear in the archives of Pier 21, in Halifax, in a short film called *In Hiding* that is used for teaching purposes in the United States, and in the anthology *Remember Us*, a compendium of thirty memoirs of hidden children in Hungary, which she co-edited. She continues to teach privately and to write whenever time permits.

EVA MARX: ONE OF THE LUCKY ONES

The only child of Eugene (Jenö) Felsenburg and Helen (Ilonka) Weisz, Eva Felsenburg Marx was born on October 21, 1937 in Brno, Czechoslovakia, a bustling industrial city in the region of Moravia, now part of the Czech Republic. Her parents, like many Jewish families at the time, had migrated from small villages in the region of Slovakia to take advantage of the economic and educational opportunities in bigger, more modernized urban centres like Brno. When Eva was born, Brno (Brünn in German) had a thriving Jewish population of about 12,000 and was home to numerous Jewish professionals and business owners like Eva's father, who was the proprietor of two fur stores.

When the German army occupied Czechoslovakia on March 16, 1939, Eva's family began their lives as fugitives. The invasion no doubt took them by surprise. Families like Eva's had enjoyed relative security since the First Czechoslovak Republic was formed out of the dissolution of the Austro-Hungarian Empire in the aftermath of World War I and were staunch supporters of the new democratic government headed by President Tomáš Garrigue Masaryk. Jews had played a key role in industry and trade in the regions of Bohemia and Moravia long before the new republic was formed in 1918. The 1849 law of free movement had allowed Jews to move out of Jewish-designated areas into cities previously forbidden to them and simultaneously opened up new ways of thinking. Jews became part of Czech-Jewish urban movements that, like Judy Abrams' family, embraced modernization and assimilated to fit in with the cultural norms of the larger Christian populace. Even Jews who continued to maintain strong ties to their Jewish roots wrote and spoke German and Czech, rather than Yiddish, and were loyal subjects of the Hapsburg Empire.

Jewish soldiers like Eva's grandfather proudly fought for their country and many died in World War I.

The First Czechoslovak Republic incorporated the provinces of Bohemia and Moravia, as well as part of Silesia, Slovakia and Subcarpathian Ruthenia that had formerly been provinces of Hungary. Czechoslovakia now included numerous ethnic groups, including Czechs, Sudeten Germans, Slovaks, Magyar (Hungarians), Ukrainian, Jewish, Polish and Roma. The new democracy under President Masaryk guaranteed freedom of conscience and religion, assured all minorities equal rights, and affirmed a separation of church and state. In 1921, there were 354,000 Jews out of a population of more than 13.5 million living in Czechoslovakia, a significant number of them in public services or professions; they also made up 30 to 40 per cent of capital investment in industry. By 1936, approximately 18 per cent of all university students in the country were Jewish. These opportunities did not necessarily extend to Jewish women, who, like Eva's mother, often had to rely on arranged marriages to advance in Czechoslovak society. Still, the republic was quick to extend the vote to women soon after its establishment in 1918, even before Great Britain and the United States.

Adolf Hitler's rise to power and plans – in direct contravention of the 1919 Treaty of Versailles – to expand Germany's borders to create a "Greater Germany" in Europe had far-reaching effects for the young Czechoslovak republic. Hitler's first move in that direction had been the annexation of Austria, known as the *Anschluss*, on March 12, 1938. His next step was to exploit the grievances of the three million *Volksdeutsche* (ethnic Germans) living in the Sudetenland, the territories along Czechoslovakia's borders with Germany and Austria, and demand that these regions be transferred to the Third Reich. Hoping to avert another major war, Britain and France decided unilaterally to cede the Sudetenland to Germany at the September 1938 Munich conference. But it did not take long for Hitler to push beyond the terms of that agreement: on March 15, 1939, the German army marched into Czechoslovakia. The western part of the country, where Brno was situated, came under direct German control. The Slovakian region of the former republic became a puppet-state governed by the pro-Nazi Hlinka's Slovak People's Party (HSSP), headed by its president, Father Jozef Tiso. In the far southeast of the republic, Hungary annexed the region of Subcarpathian Ruthenia, where Eva's maternal grandparents lived.

In an instant, life for the Jews of Bohemia and Moravia rapidly deteriorated. In Brno and the capital city of Prague synagogues were destroyed, businesses and properties were confiscated, and Jews were isolated as pariahs. On November 16, 1941, one thousand Jews from Brno were interned in the military barracks of Spielberg Castle before being transported to a ghetto in Minsk, Belarus. They were then taken to a nearby forest and massacred. Just over a week later, on November 24, 1941, the Nazis established a Jewish ghetto and concentration camp in the old fortress town of Terezin (Theresienstadt in German), forty-eight kilometres away from Prague, and the mass deportation of Czechoslovak Jews began soon after. In total, between November 1941 and May 1945, about 140,000 Jews from Prague, Brno and other towns were sent first to Terezin and from there almost 90,000 were transported to death camps in occupied Poland. Close to 30,000 more died in Terezin itself. Some 15,000 of the Jews who were sent to Terezin were children.

Following the Nazi invasion, Eva's parents moved quickly to protect their young child and sent her to her maternal grandparents' home in Vráble, a small town in the region of Slovakia that had been annexed by Hungary in the 1939 partition. To avoid being caught for deportation, Eva's parents kept on the move. Over the next five years, young Eva was for the most part unaware of the danger that surrounded her as she participated in village life at her grandparents' home, cared for by her extended family and her beloved maid, Marka. There were only 250 Jews living in Vráble, but they enjoyed a vibrant, traditional Jewish life. Eva fondly remembers her grandmother's home cooking, the Sabbath meals and playing with the village children. She also occasionally saw her mother or went to visit extended family in Budapest. At the same time, conditions in the rest of Slovakia were not much better than they were in the German Protectorate of Bohemia and Moravia. Slovakia had instituted racial laws known as the Jewish Code in 1941 that stripped anyone of Jewish descent of their rights and excluded them from public life. From March to October 1942, while Eva was being sheltered in her grandparents' home, close to 70,000 Slovakian Jews were transported to death camps in Poland such as Sobibor, Majdanek and Auschwitz.

In the spring of 1944, as Slovak resistance to the Nazis and Tiso's pro-fascist government began to gain momentum, Eva's father arranged a hiding place for the family in Nitra, one of Slovakia's oldest cities, and arranged for Eva to be smuggled the short distance from Vráble to Nitra. People in Slovakia knew that the Soviet Red Army was pushing the war front westward and he no doubt felt that it would be safe for the family to wait for what they hoped was an imminent German surrender. Whatever his reasoning, that spring of 1944, Eva was re-united with her parents and the move saved her life. Not long after, in May 1944, Hungary began deporting Jews in the Hungarian countryside to Auschwitz.

Eva and her parents, along with two other families, waited out the war for another seven months hidden in an apartment. When Soviet troops liberated the area in April 1945 there were close to 1,400 Jews living under false documents or protected in Nitra's famous *yeshiva* (a Jewish Orthodox institution for the study of traditional texts): but not all were as lucky as Eva and her family. In September 1944, while they were in hiding, Hlinka Guards continued to diligently hunt for hidden Jews. Three hundred Jews in Nitra who were hiding in apartments like Eva's were found and sent to Auschwitz.

When the war finally ended in May 1945, Eva's mother returned to Vráble to find that all of her immediate family had been killed. Some of Eva's paternal relatives managed to survive the war by hiding in Budapest, much like Judy Abrams and her family. In 1945, exiled president Edvard Beneš returned to Czechoslovakia from London, where he had been supporting the Allies, and became the head of the Second Republic of Czechoslovakia, restoring democracy once again. Eva and her family moved back to Brno where her father re-established his business and Eva returned to school to be with other children her age. Yet life did not return to normal for most European Jews in this post-war period. The pain of returning to homes and towns where so many family members and loved ones had been killed was devastating. This trauma and upheaval was exacerbated for Jews living in areas controlled by the Soviets; in February 1948, the Czechoslovak Communist Party staged a coup d'état that ended democracy in that country for decades. Privately owned businesses were nationalized almost immediately and Eva's father once again lost everything he had built up.

In 1948, Jews in Czechoslovakia once more found themselves looking for a safe haven. The newly established State of Israel, which had declared independence on May 14, 1948, was encouraging Holocaust survivors to immigrate to their ancestral home and help develop the country. In Vráble, most of the eighty-seven Jews who had returned from the war moved to Israel; in Nitra, too, the majority of the six hundred surviving Jews left for Israel in 1949. Zionist organizations such as the secular socialist youth movement Hashomer Hatzair were especially active in recruiting and organizing immigration to Israel. These organizations set up training centres that instilled in youth a strong sense of Jewish identity by focusing on social equality, teaching Hebrew songs and Jewish history, and preparing youth for a new existence in Israel with vigorous physical activity. Eva, for example, describes going to a winter camp organized by Hashomer Hatzair.

Along with many other Holocaust survivors, Eva's family made plans to immigrate to Israel to start life anew. At the last moment, however, feeling that his skills as a furrier would be more valuable in a cold climate, her father changed his mind and decided to move the family to Canada. Sponsored by Eva's aunt Hedwig, her father's older sister, they arrived in Canada in 1949, the very same year as Judy Abrams and her parents. Despite never crossing paths, Eva, like Judy, turned twelve years old on the boat to Canada and settled with her parents in Montreal, where many Jewish immigrants were establishing themselves in the garment industry.

The importance of family plays a key role in Eva's memoir. Her devotion to her parents as they struggle to establish a fur business in Montreal is remarkable when considering she herself had so many adjustments to contend with. While her exhausted parents worked long hours making and mending fur coats, Eva also worked hard, excelling in school and building close, long-lasting friendships. In 1956, after graduating from high school, Eva, like Judy Abrams, completed an accelerated teacher's program at MacDonald College in Ste. Anne de Bellevue in Quebec. During this time, she also met her future husband, Herbert Marx, who went on to have an exciting career as a lawyer, becoming minister of justice and attorney general of Quebec from 1985 to 1988, and a justice of the Quebec Superior Court from 1989 to 2007. Eva and Herb married in 1959. While she was teaching at Elmgrove Elementary School in Montreal, Eva also went to night school at Sir George Williams (now Concordia University) and completed her BA in 1962. She continued her studies and received her master's degree in sociology from the Université de Montréal in 1987. She gave birth to her two children, Robert, who was born in 1965, and Sarah, who was born in 1970, and is now the proud grandmother of four grandchildren: Ella, Hannah, Harry and David. Eva's dedication to her own mother in her last years of life remains an example of the generous spirit that emerges throughout her memoir.

～

When we read the memoirs of child survivors like Eva Marx and Judy Abrams it is important to keep in mind that Jewish children in Nazi-occupied Europe had, for the most part, very little opportunity to escape death and even less chance of being able to tell their stories before they left the world. The stories of survival that we are fortunate enough to have are not only about the past – they bring with them the message of respect for life and freedom that are as necessary and relevant today as they were in the period these authors are writing about. Judy Abrams and Eva Marx's willingness to share their memoirs with subsequent generations reminds us that we are all memory keepers for the many hidden children who did not have the opportunity to share their stories with us.

Mia Spiro
York University
2011

LIST OF SOURCES AND SUGGESTIONS FOR FURTHER READING:

Abrams, Judy and Evi Blaikie, eds. *Remember Us: A Collection of Memories from Hungarian Children of the Holocaust.* The Hungarian Children of New York. Bloomington, IN: Authorhouse, 2010.

Bergen, Doris. *The Holocaust: A Concise History.* Lanham, MD: Rowman and Littlefield, 2009.

Braham, Randolph. *The Politics of Genocide: The Holocaust in Hungary.* New York: Columbia University Press, 1981.

Braham, Randolph and Scott Miller, eds. *The Nazis' Last Victims: The Holocaust in Hungary.* Detroit: Wayne State University Press, 1998.

Case, Holly. "Territorial Revision and the Holocaust: Hungary and Slovakia during World War II." In *Lessons and Legacies VIII: From Generation to Generation.* Ed. Doris Bergen. Evanston, IL: Northwestern University Press, 2008, 222–246.

Dwork, Deborah. *Children with a Star: Jewish Youth in Nazi Europe.* New Haven, CT: Yale University Press, 1991.

Krell, Robert. "Psychological Reverberations of the Holocaust in the Lives of Child Survivors." Washington, DC: United States Holocaust Memorial Museum, 1997.

Marks, Jane, ed. *The Hidden Children: The Secret Survivors of the Holocaust.* New York: Ballantine, 1993.

Paldiel, Mordecai. "Fear and Comfort: The Plight of Hidden Jewish Children in Wartime-Poland." *Holocaust and Genocide Studies* 6:4 (1991): 397–413.

Specter, Shmuel and Geoffrey Wigoder, eds. *Encyclopedia of Jewish Life Before and During the Holocaust.* Vols 1–3. New York: New York University Press, 2001.

Reiter, Andrea. *Children of the Holocaust.* London: Vallentine Mitchell, 2005.

Rothkirchen, Livia. *The Jews of Bohemia and Moravia: Facing the Holocaust.* Lincoln, NE: University of Nebraska Press, 2005.

Tec, Nechama. "A Historical Perspective: Tracing the History of the Hidden-Children Experience." In *The Hidden Children: The Secret Survivors of the Holocaust.* Ed. Jane Marks. New York: Ballantine, 1993, 273–291.

United States Holocaust Memorial Museum. "Hidden Children"; "The Holocaust in Slovakia"; "Hungary after German Occupation." *Holocaust Encyclopedia.* http://www.ushmm.org/wlc/en. Accessed on March 15, 2011.

Tenuous Threads

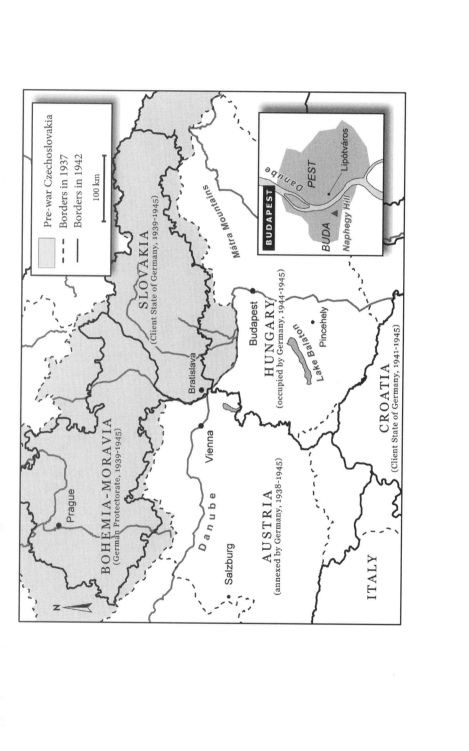

Pre-war Czechoslovakia

--- Borders in 1937
— Borders in 1942

100 km

BOHEMIA-MORAVIA
(German Protectorate, 1939-1945)

Prague

SLOVAKIA
(Client State of Germany, 1939-1945)

Mátra Mountains

Bratislava

Budapest

HUNGARY
(occupied by Germany, 1944-1945)

Lake Balaton

Pincehely

Danube

Vienna

AUSTRIA
(annexed by Germany, 1938-1945)

Salzburg

CROATIA
(Client State of Germany, 1941-1945)

ITALY

BUDAPEST

Danube

PEST

Lipótváros

BUDA

Naphegy Hill

Judy Abrams' Family Tree*

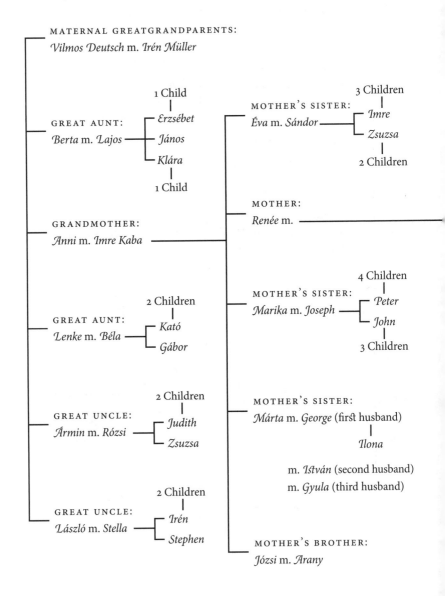

MATERNAL GREATGRANDPARENTS:
Vilmos Deutsch m. *Irén Müller*

GREAT AUNT:
Berta m. *Lajos*

1 Child
|
Erzsébet
János
Klára
|
1 Child

MOTHER'S SISTER:
Éva m. *Sándor*

3 Children
|
Imre
Zsuzsa
|
2 Children

GRANDMOTHER:
Anni m. *Imre Kaba*

MOTHER:
Renée m. ─────

GREAT AUNT:
Lenke m. *Béla*

2 Children
|
Kató
Gábor

MOTHER'S SISTER:
Marika m. *Joseph*

4 Children
|
Peter
John
|
3 Children

GREAT UNCLE:
Ármin m. *Rózsi*

2 Children
|
Judith
Zsuzsa

MOTHER'S SISTER:
Márta m. *George* (first husband)
|
Ilona

m. *István* (second husband)
m. *Gyula* (third husband)

GREAT UNCLE:
László m. *Stella*

2 Children
|
Irén
Stephen

MOTHER'S BROTHER:
Józsi m. *Arany*

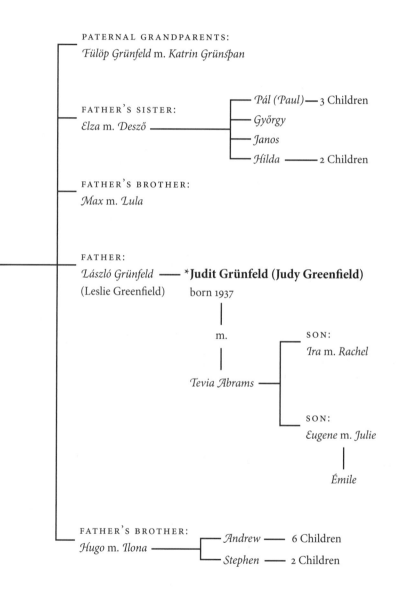

PATERNAL GRANDPARENTS:
Fülöp Grünfeld m. *Katrin Grünspan*

FATHER'S SISTER:
Elza m. *Desző* ———
— *Pál (Paul)* — 3 Children
— *György*
— *Janos*
— *Hilda* ——— 2 Children

FATHER'S BROTHER:
Max m. *Lula*

FATHER:
László Grünfeld ——— **Judit Grünfeld (Judy Greenfield)*
(Leslie Greenfield)   born 1937

m.

Tevia Abrams ———
SON:
Ira m. *Rachel*

SON:
Eugene m. *Julie*

Émile

FATHER'S BROTHER:
Hugo m. *Ilona* ———
— *Andrew* — 6 Children
— *Stephen* — 2 Children

"I lost two cities, lovely ones. And, vaster,
  some realms I owned, two rivers, a continent…"

"…the art of losing's not too hard to master…"

– Elizabeth Bishop, *One Art*

For my parents, Leslie and Renée Greenfield, who did not lose me,
and to Tevia who helped me find myself.

Chestnut Boulevard

We were walking along the Fasor, a broad avenue lined with wild chestnut trees near the city park. My mother and I walked hand in hand under the lush green trees decked out in their festive spring finery, white and pink blossom clusters that looked like miniature Christmas trees. It was a street I knew well. In a few weeks the blossoms would drift to the sidewalk to create a soft pink carpet, which I loved to shuffle in. Later, the flowers would be replaced by round, spiky green pods that weighed down the branches until early fall, when they too dropped to the pavement and released shiny mahogany chestnuts. I collected them by the bagful to hoard in a deep drawer all winter. There, they'd gradually lose their sheen and begin to wrinkle, wizened faces of old men, discarded and eventually replaced by the new crop of the following spring. But there would be no wild chestnuts for me in the fall. It was April 1944 in Budapest. The German army had taken over Hungary on March 19. I was seven years old.

My mother held my hand tighter than necessary, although I was not likely to rush heedlessly into the road. To the few pedestrians who passed us, we must have seemed inconspicuous: a dark-haired woman in a tailored, grey tweed suit and a little girl in a pale-blue knitted dress. Two large matching bows attached my thick braids to each other like twin butterflies' wings propelling me onward. My mother and I both carried light coats draped over our arms. It was quite warm for April, not unusual to want to walk coatless in the sun. Those who saw us would not guess that this was a dangerous thing to do. The coats, so casually turned inside out, bore the compulsory yellow cloth Star of David sewn onto all our outer clothing, branding us Jews.[1]

"Why should I hide the star? I'm proud to be Jewish," I had announced, ignorant of the ominous implications of being seen in the street with the telltale star. Usually, I was obedient and my occasional bouts of verbal bravado simply reinforced the admiration of the adults around me. I was the precocious, much-cherished child of well-to-do parents.

How had my parents impressed upon me the importance of denying my identity, the need to maintain that I was a Christian girl called Ilona Papp, not the Jewish Judit Grünfeld? I had always liked to play make-believe, but somehow they made me understand that this game was real. I never gave away my secret. In fact, I wanted so desperately to believe that I was this other, more desirable child, that I don't recall longing for my parents. Eventually I believed that they and the past we had shared were objectionable, shameful and even worse, a sin. Folding my coat inside out was just the first step down this road.

$\sim$

I was born in Budapest on April 28, 1937 to Renée (née Kaba) and László Grünfeld. My mother's ancestors, the Deutsch-Müller family, had lived in Budapest since the nineteenth century. My father's family, who had acquired their wealth as wine merchants, had arrived more recently from northeastern Hungary. I was an only child from

---

1 For information on the Star of David, as well as on other major organizations; significant historical events and people; geographical locations; religious and cultural terms; and foreign-language words and expressions contained in the text, please see the glossary.

a middle-class family. I had previously been enrolled in Montessori nursery school and had started Grade 1 at the local elementary school on Sziv utca (Heart Street) before the Germans invaded Hungary. Because of the Nazi takeover, I never finished the school year.

My father was actively involved with the Hungarian Zionist Organization and, unlike other Hungarian Jews, he did not lull himself into a false sense of security, trusting that the "civilized" Germans and Hungarians would never harm the Jews. He believed the unbelievable stories of persecution told by the refugees from Nazi-occupied countries; he believed even the inconceivable accounts of concentration camps that the few escaped inmates had brought with them. That spring my father had managed to procure false documents for me. Were those documents copied or forged? In any case, they were my entry into the Christian Hungarian community. With the help of Mária Babar, a devout Catholic who had previously worked for our family, it was arranged for me to hide with the Ursuline nuns.

My mother had made a courageous and painful decision by taking this walk with me under the festive wild chestnuts toward the convent of the Ursuline nuns on Stefánia Street near the Városliget, the city park where I had played with my nanny only a few months before. My mother rang the outer bell on the gate of the tall, black iron railing that surrounded the convent. Behind it was a garden, where I seem to remember yellow dandelions dotting the shaggy grass that looked as though it badly needed a trim. When I recently managed to contact the Hungarian Ursuline nuns, they sent me the photograph of the convent building as it was in Budapest in 1944. My memory of the iron grill railing was accurate.

On the day my mother and I arrived at the Ursuline Mother House a strange woman in a black floor-length gown opened the gate. Only a patch of her face was visible under the stiff white band across her forehead to which a starched white bib-like collar was attached. There was no glimpse of hair under the black silk veil flowing from the band to below her shoulders and secured by a pin at the top of her head.

It was the first time I had ever seen a nun this close up. My stomach seemed to constrict around a pebble I hadn't swallowed. This is a feeling I remember distinctly, a sensation that returns whenever I confront an unavoidable crisis. She must have smiled as her hands escaped from the full sleeves of her ample dress to reach for mine because when I followed her along the path toward the yellow stucco two-storey villa, that pebble in my middle began to dissolve.

Surely my mother waved as she turned from the gate that closed behind me. We would not see each other again for more than a year. How did she say goodbye? She may have said something that ended in *pipikém* (my little chicken), her favourite endearment for me in Hungarian. I only remember feeling strangely relieved as she released me to follow on my own behind my new companion. From this black-clad woman's waist swung a string of large beads ending in a cross that bounced at every lively step. When she opened the front door she had addressed me for the first time by my new name, "Ilona," or its diminutive, "Ili." Nobody would call me "Judit" or "Jutka" or "Juditka" for almost a year. The game now began in earnest. I was to become Ilona Papp, a Catholic child temporarily separated from her parents in the Hungarian countryside. I had crisp white documents to prove my identity: a birth certificate and a baptismal certificate.

The interior of the convent was shuttered and the furniture in the large rooms was covered with white sheets, just like in our apartment in Budapest when we left for summer vacation by Lake Balaton or in the Mátra Mountains. The Mother Superior had moved most of the nuns and the students who boarded with them to the country at Pincehely in Transdanubia, to be safe from the impending bombing of the capital, and I would soon be moved there, too. The Mother Superior's concern proved to be well-founded. As I found out many years later, in June 1944 the building on Stefánia Street was destroyed by bombs and only the chapel, where the few remaining nuns took shelter, stayed intact. I was already safe in the country.

That night, I ate a cold supper by myself in the large, unoccupied kitchen at a wooden table watched by the nun who had opened the gate. I slept in a room all by myself in a large bed under a soft, white, cotton comforter, not pink and light-blue silk like mine at home. The next day, I met a short, chubby, cheerful older nun who would instruct me in the prayers and some of the essential rituals: the Ave Maria and the Lord's Prayer, a few questions and answers in the catechism, and the use of the rosary. The rosary she gave me, made of tiny white pearly beads, eventually saved my life. I learned easily the words and gestures that would mark me as a particularly religious child. This was the key to the new game. Only I was no longer pretending. I had assumed the part I was to play.

I also received a small black prayer book that I still keep at the back of one of my drawers, as unused as the handkerchiefs under which it lies, a reminder of the self I had abandoned after the war.

Was it then that I met the Mother Superior? She was a tall woman whose silk veil was even finer than the other nun's. Did I just imagine that as she drew me to her and I let myself be pulled into the generous folds of black cloth, my face touched the silver figure on the smooth wooden cross and that I drew back from the cold contact?

Before one of the sisters and I boarded a train for the brief journey from Budapest to the country, scissors snipped the threads securing the yellow star on my sky-blue coat. I didn't protest anymore that I was proud to be Jewish. The Sister presented our documents to the Hungarian gendarmes with the rooster plumes on their helmets. Called the *csendőr* (gendarmes), they were notorious for finding, tormenting and deporting Jews in the Hungarian countryside. "Dicsértessék a Jézus Krisztust!" (Praised be Jesus Christ!) is what they must have said with respect to the nun and probably looked fondly at the sweet Christian girl in her unbranded sky-blue coat. It all seemed so easy. There was now only Ilona, Ili, and nobody would spit at her and call her "Büdös Zsidó" (Stinking Jew) as one of my father's labourers had done to the other me. She did not wear a yellow star. She had become a "real" Hungarian girl.

I remember a long, unvarnished wooden table set for the afternoon snack of thickly buttered, crusty country bread and mugs of coffee with milk in the convent garden when we arrived. No more cocoa in the porcelain cup with the blue forget-me-nots that I'd had at home. I was ready for this new treat until I noticed a hard leathery layer forming on the surface of the drink. I hated the "skin" of hot milk. Was this unchristian? I closed my eyes and, almost choking on the slimy film, gulped down the warm liquid without pausing for breath.

The Saving Beads

As I walked under the sweet-scented linden trees, my bare feet welcomed each painful pebble. I mumbled the recently learned Ave Maria, fingering my rosary, the circlet of tiny, white beads ending in a silver crucifix. It was just the right size for small fingers to move along, a prayer recited for each grain. I was good at make-believe – so good that I had made my previous, Jewish self fade, receding into forbidden recesses of my mind. The pride I had once felt in wearing the Star of David was replaced by the satisfaction of repeating the appropriate prayers for each white bead of my new rosary.

The convent garden at Pincehely was crisscrossed by paths of small, sharp red pebbles. I was voluntarily doing penance for the sins of the previous week, like the martyred saints. Not THE LIE about who I really was, but others, more in keeping with my current beliefs. There were the sinful glances at the boys with whom my new friend, Mari, and I shared a bedroom. A venial sin for me to watch as they briefly lowered their pyjamas for our admiration. Even though the act was initiated by our male roommates, it was a foolhardy gesture that could have betrayed their secret, the one all four of us shared. They were circumcised. We never spoke about our Jewish identity, not even with our best friends.

"Ouch!" – a pointed red pebble nearly pierced the tender sole of my city-bred foot. I welcomed the pain, proof of my sacrifice for the love of the beautiful blond Mother Mary with her rosy infant, enveloped in a soft blue cloak, painted on the ceiling of the chapel. "Ave Maria," I recited fervently, hoping she would excuse me for having left my doll, Anikó, out in the rain; for not eating the slippery, cooked green peppers served at dinner last night; for vanity when I wanted Sister to attach my braids with a shiny, wide satin bow, not narrow navy ribbons; for envy when Ági's handwriting drew more praise than mine; for sloth, too, not taking the trouble to write better. "Ouch!" Again. I fingered the next bead. Serves me right. "Ave…"

It was July, a wonderful, warm, sunny month, a time for picking cherries and tasting the soft inner stems of the grasses I called wild wheat. I had been in the convent in Pincehely for three months now, learning a little arithmetic and spelling in the morning and spending many more hours reading the stories of saints whose pictures my new friends and I avidly collected and swapped. The patron saints I had selected were St. Theresa of Avila and St. Francis of Assisi. My most treasured picture was of St. Francis scattering food to the flocks of birds that surrounded him. We were also taught the correct responses to the questions of the catechism and vied with each other in repeating the answers without a flaw.

The sister who was in charge of this part of our education was kind but not pretty. I could tell, even though the white band across her forehead attached to her starched white bib hid much of her face. Her hair was covered by a white veil, not black like the older nuns. She was a novice, not yet fully a nun. Brown eyebrows and eyelashes hinted that she was dark, not blond like the painting in the chapel. I would become a nun, I decided, and when I shared my vocation with the sisters they responded with smiles of approval on their faces, tiny ovals of skin framed in white and black. The desire to accumulate further merit motivated me to undertake my pilgrimage on the stony paths of the garden, passing from bead to bead, from Ave to Ave, only occasionally punctuated by cries of surprised pain.

It was fall when my daily penitent pilgrimages on the red gravel paths of the convent garden came to an end with the sudden arrival of Mária. My parents had entrusted me to her care when they left Budapest on a journey that eventually led them to Bergen-Belsen concentration camp. Mother Superior had contacted Mária and asked her to take me with her to Budapest, where I would be safer. The German SS, Hitler's black-uniformed security force, had been alerted to the presence of Jews in convents and monasteries. They were committing atrocities against the Jews they discovered and brutally punishing those who dared to shelter them. We were to return to Budapest by train the next day, packing only a small suitcase with the most essential belongings and my smiling celluloid doll, Anikó. Whatever else my parents had given to the nuns on my behalf would be lost forever.

I regretted leaving the convent and the familiar garden surrounded by lush green fields and orchards. I would miss the white stucco house with its narrow corridors where the nuns whooshed by in their dark habits, the wooden beads of their rosaries clicking at every hurried step. I would no longer sit in awe in the chapel on Sunday mornings, lulled by the music of the liturgy, admiring the intricate embroidery on the back of the cassock of the priest officiating at the altar, inhaling the perfume of incense wafted in silver censers by the village boys whose white smocks were bordered in lace like the tablecloths of the home I had to forget.

The train ride to Budapest was very different from the one that had brought me to the country. Then, I had sat comfortably in a compartment accompanied by the sister who elicited a respectful "Praised be Jesus Christ!" from passengers and officials alike as they made the sign of the cross, touching their foreheads and shoulders in the form of a cross. Now, we stood in the aisle among peasant women in ample gathered skirts of many colours. Everyone carried some luggage. There were bulging suitcases fastened with string and baskets of food containing fat rods of salami and giant wheels of country bread wrapped in checkered cloth. There were even chickens and geese, their feet tied, tucked in baskets, clucking and quacking all the way to the city. I held onto Mária's hand with my left hand and clutched the beads of my rosary in my right, secure in the earthly protection of one woman and the heavenly intervention of the other.

It was 1944 and World War II was drawing to a close, but Hungary continued to support the losing German army. Ferenc Szálasi, the fascist dictator of the country, was still enthusiastically helping the effort to eradicate the Jews of Europe. His loyal troops, the Arrow Cross brigade (Nyilas), assisted the German SS in rounding up Jews into cattle cars and sending most of them to the death camps at Auschwitz and Birkenau. The brigade, a haven for unemployed and under-educated young men, roamed the streets of Budapest arresting Jews who transgressed the imposed curfew, failed to wear the compulsory yellow star or possessed false "Aryan" documents. They relished wielding their power over women, children and old people, proudly sporting their emblem – an armband marked with intersecting arrows that formed the arrow cross – as a symbol of allegiance to Szálasi, Hitler and death.

By the time Mária and I took the train from Pincehely to Budapest nearly all the Jews in the Hungarian countryside had been deported and Budapest was the only capital in Europe with any considerable Jewish population. These Jews managed to exist in buildings designated as Jewish houses, marked with Stars of David. The apartments were shared by several families, mostly made up of women, children and the elderly since able-bodied men had already been sent in special *munkaszolgálat*, forced labour detachments to assist the army at the eastern front of the war.

How much did I know about all this? Probably very little, perhaps some fragments I had overheard. As Mária and I stood in the cramped train, I was also ignorant of the fate of my parents, now in Bergen-Belsen, the concentration camp in Germany where Anne Frank had spent her last days. I was fortunate to be sheltered by Mária, my grandmother, Nagyi, and my mother's sister, Aunt Marika, who were already in Mária's tiny studio apartment when we arrived. Mária had rescued them when the woman who had agreed (for a price) to shelter them in her home on the outskirts of Budapest became frightened and made them leave her house in the middle of the night.

In the crowded apartment Mária surrounded me with love and even playfulness that made up for my grandmother's stern silence and Aunt Marika's quiet sadness. I don't remember what their new names were, but they too had written proof attesting to their "Aryan" origin. We never talked of the past but lived in a present fraught with dangerous secrets. My grandmother tried to uphold high standards of behaviour, order and cleanliness. War and persecution didn't lessen her expectations. She still reminded me firmly not to use a dishtowel to wipe my hands when hand towels were available.

It was Mária I loved best. She was affectionate and funny and took me to church with her on Sundays at the bottom of Naphegy (Sun Mountain), where we lived. I had grown to relish the perfumed incense and the melodic refrains of the Latin mass. My grandmother frowned on the daily rosary sessions I shared with Mária. Outward manifestation of any faith seemed to her to be in bad taste, the transgression of a personal code of conduct. This included my holy beads. She held them at arm's length if I left them lying around, as though they were not quite clean.

I relegated my previous life and my parents to a sinful past, in which they, and even I, could be held responsible for the crucifixion of Christ. I had heard horrendous accusations against Jews – cheating, greed and even sacrificial murder. No wonder I was glad to be able to dissociate myself from such ancestors.

My First and Only Christmas

Christmas came and Mária bought a real Christmas tree, taking up much of the cramped single room in which my grandmother, Aunt Marika, Mária and I all lived. It was enveloped in gossamer strands of angel's hair and glittering tinsel. I was looking forward to tasting the foil-wrapped traditional Hungarian Christmas candies hanging on its branches and lighting the candles poised at the tip of each. Presents were piled under the tree, the ones I was going to open and those I had stitched and drawn, cut and pasted, wrapping them carefully for family and friends. It was going to be better than a birthday party.

Finally, on Christmas Eve, we finished our festive meal. I don't remember what it was, though I'm sure it was not the traditional goose. I seem to remember there were some horseshoe-shaped poppy seed and sweet ground walnut-filled cakes that Jews called *beigli* and gentiles called *patkó*. Shopping for food had become a challenge as the Soviet army approached Budapest. Meat and sugar were strictly rationed and available only on the presentation of little green squares of the ration card, each specifically marked with an allotted amount. I now wonder whether Mária had dared to apply for ration cards for her "houseguests." Whatever its source, it was a splendid feast. Would we have enjoyed it even more if we had realized then that this would be our last real meal for months?

When the candles were lit I was in ecstasy. I sang my favourite Hungarian Christmas carol, "Mennyből az angyal leszállt a földre" (The angel descended from heaven to earth…). I sang lustily with Mária and her guests. My favourite person was the chubby "Auntie Superintendent," who was in charge of our building. She smiled at me warmly. Auntie approved of my devotion to the rosary and the collection of saints' pictures I treasured. My beautiful, elegant aunt – a symphony in muted colours of wool and silk – was tone-deaf in any liturgy. She mouthed the words off-key, "Lássátok! Lássátok!" (Behold! Behold!). My grandmother, dressed in black, in mourning since the death of her husband many years ago, stood erect, unable to do more than open and close her lips silently on the words. She was not a devout person. Her Judaism was a quiet faith expressed in the observation of dietary laws, the special meals celebrating each holiday, and the lighting of candles on Friday night and on death anniversaries.

Before we had a chance to utter the last refrains, there was a resounding "Bang!" followed by the shrieking of air-raid sirens throughout the city. From Naphegy in Buda, where Mária's apartment was located, we could see the bridges exploding like fireworks across the Danube. From Castle Hill, where the royal castle loomed over the scene of devastation, cannons boomed. Machine guns staccatoed. Hand grenades exploded. Windows shattered. Airplanes buzzed above us in clusters.

We took refuge in the basement, a make-do bomb shelter. The women of the house had been preparing for this event by partitioning the large space for storage. There were mattresses on old iron bedsteads, jars of preserves on the shelves – including duck, fried and packed in jars filled with duck fat – and tall brown jute sacks of flour, onions and potatoes. All this was in readiness for a time when we would not be able to surface to procure food from outside.

My Christmas presents, those I was to have received and the ones I wanted to distribute, remained upstairs to be buried under the rubble of the house, which gradually collapsed over our heads. The Siege of Budapest had begun on my first and only Christmas.

~

From Christmas 1944 until February 1945 we seldom emerged, miraculously safe while the building fell to pieces above us. In the basement, Auntie Superintendent and I had become great friends. She was a reliable dispenser of hard candy, even during the Siege of Budapest.

Years later history would testify that World War II was drawing to a close at that time. I later found out that Naphegy, where we lived, was the last hold-out of the German and Hungarian forces against the Soviet Red Army. As the Soviets closed in, the sound of their arrival was deafening. Electricity had failed almost as soon as we entered the cellar, where we lived mostly by the light of candles and petroleum lamps. The glass chimneys set above round containers of petroleum protected the flickering flames of felt wicks and channelled smoke and foul smells up toward the exposed beams of the ceiling.

I recall two memorable occasions when we climbed the stairs into the light of day from the dimly lit cellar. The first must have been in mid-January. The dirty snow was littered with rubble and fragments of broken glass from the shattered house. We stood with our backs to the stucco building, which by then had been battered by cannon, bombs and grenades. My eyes and those of the frightened collection of men and women obliged to leave the dubious safety of our shelter were riveted on a small group of young men facing us menacingly. Somebody had reported that there were Jews in the building, hidden by some of the tenants. It was their purpose to find them.

The men did not wear uniforms. I don't remember if they carried weapons, but the dreaded Arrow Cross armbands were intimidating enough. Numerous accounts confirm that even while the Soviet troops approached Budapest to finally defeat the Germans, while the city lay in ruins and the bridges spanning the Danube were destroyed, these gangs still roamed the streets to capture any remaining Jews. In the winter of 1944, Jewish victims were lined up on the banks of the Danube and machine gunned until they disappeared into the icy waters. The trains carrying Jews to foreign concentration camps were no longer rumbling, yet the Arrow Cross continued to enact their own version of the "Final Solution to the Jewish Problem."

In spite of my recently acquired faith and firm belief in my new identity, there must have been a sudden apprehension that somewhere underneath Ilona Papp was a different and endangered person. I felt the terror of my grandmother and my aunt, and the anger of Mária who hovered close to us. In spite of their proximity, I remember standing alone in my grey winter coat with its blue lined hood. I had inherited it from my cousin Zsuzsa, who always looked particularly well-dressed and never wore out her clothes. The occasional hand-me-downs from her were very special. I loved the grey coat, but suddenly felt awkward in its bulk. I felt clumsy and vulnerable as the young men ("hoodlums" Mária called them in secret) examined the papers that were supposed to prove our Aryan origin. Slowly, one by one. My aunt and grandmother were given long, piercing stares as their new names were verified. A sigh of relief, when the documents were handed back without comment. My grandmother's icy blue eyes and my aunt's elegant profile aroused no suspicion. It was my turn.

"This birth certificate seems very new," one of them commented.

"Of course," my grandmother spoke up with authority born out of habit and desperation, "in other times, we did not have to carry around our documents to prove who we were...." (Did she add, "to every stranger"?) One of the men looked at me too carefully and conferred with his colleagues.

"The child looks Jewish," he pronounced with disdain.

The lump of dread in the pit of my stomach is a clear memory. I remember standing very still and separate, waiting.... And then, Auntie Superintendent's voice boomed over the sporadic gunfire around us.

"Shame on you! This child is a devout Catholic. She prays more than you, you punk!"

In spite of the sounds of battle, silence descended on the panic-stricken band of survivors from the shelter. (I later found out that most of them were Jews in hiding.) There was a long, long silence until my papers were wordlessly handed back to Nagyi. I was saved by the beads.

The Saving Cry

That January 1945 – a cold month in Hungary, especially in the unheated cellar – I had had my brush with death by firing squad.

Not all the inhabitants of our tenuous shelter were equally fortunate. There was an elderly couple (they were probably in their fifties but seemed old to me) who occupied a small "room" at the far end of the cellar, a space previously used for storing wood or coal. They rarely spoke. Keeping to themselves, they exuded an aura of faded elegance in shades of grey: hair, skin, clothes and the sadness that characterized their slow silent movements. Under the layers of outerwear to protect her from the cold, I imagined the lady wearing a simple dress of soft material in muted colours. She wore her hair in two wing-like rolls, held in place by fine, brown bone combs, a style fashionable in the 1940s. Like my Aunt Marika, she never looked untidy. It was as though their previous life of ease and good taste had followed them into the recesses of the dingy cellar.

Relieved that we had escaped the ominous visit of the Arrow Cross, I was bundled off to our corner. There, in relative safety, I began to hear shouts and screams from the back of the basement. The outer door then slammed while the sound of continuing sobs lingered. A curious child, I listened to the whispered conversations and gradually pieced together the story. The "hoodlums" had not stopped at examining documents and faces. Hungarian gentiles were seldom circumcised. After the outdoor inspection, the Arrow Cross thugs led the elderly couple back into the cellar where the dignified gentleman was told to lower his pants. Their suspicions confirmed, they marched him off to join a contingent of Jews who had been "caught" and made to march toward the Danube, a certain death by firing squad. But before taking him away, the men had done something bad to his wife, to the elegant lady at the back of the cellar. This was a secret nobody allowed me to share. After this event, her hair was no longer carefully rolled on top of her head and the men's clothes she put on did not give off the faint aroma of perfume.

Strangely, this story has a fortunate ending. One day, two young men arrived at the house carrying on a makeshift stretcher the old man we had taken for dead. In his younger years, he had been an Olympic swimmer. As the victims were lined up along the banks of the river facing the Arrow Cross firing squad, he decided to take a chance. Before the bullets could reach him, he jumped backward into the icy Danube. Through the ice floes he swam to the shore, where a woman found him naked and bruised but alive. She nursed him until he was ready to be returned to his wife by the young men. Who were the young men who carried him back? Sons? Friends? Neighbours? They asked for no compensation.

In her eternal black clothes, Nagyi began to look like an old Hungarian peasant. She bustled about baking yeastless bread, much like our ancestors did in the story of the Exodus from Egypt. Only now there was no Land of Canaan in sight. She still tried to maintain a semblance of discipline and refused to give in to my requests for pieces of the fresh loaves. Warm bread was bad for the stomach, according to the dictates of some obscure rule of health. She was the one who carefully portioned out the remaining bits of duck and goose preserved in jars of yellow fat and the ever-shrinking stores of onions and potatoes in jute sacks.

Deprivation and anxiety did not improve her naturally stern disposition, nor did it make me into a more pliant child. I prayed with

Mária and Auntie Superintendent, charming them with my faith. But with my grandmother I was demanding and capricious. We were not well-suited to each other and needed the constant intervention of my gentle Aunt Marika or Mária, who usually took my side and cajoled me into a better mood by calling me "Kis Kutyám" (her little puppy) or other funny endearments. She managed to mollify my grandmother, too.

The thin walls did not muffle the sounds of battle. Bombs and cannon balls crashed into the ruins of the house above us, and sharp bits of shrapnel embedded themselves into the walls. Hand grenades were hurled into the garden as the gunfire came ever nearer. We had mixed feelings toward the Soviet liberators, who did not have a sterling reputation. Stories of looting and more terrible things done to women circulated. Besides, the closer the battle lines came to our house, the less secure our lodgings became. We were only barely below ground level.

In the garden adjacent to ours was a real bomb shelter, dug deep and lined with cement. It was decided that we, the cellar-dwellers, would try to stay there during the day and return at night, when the fighting usually slackened. As we emerged from our dark hovel, we found the icy ground covered in debris. We stumbled and slipped, crawling, keeping low, occasionally lying down as some manner of fire or shell whizzed overhead. Bullets glanced off the ice mounds and I seem to recall seeing bloodstains on the no-longer-white snow. I cried and begged to go back to the relative safety of the basement, but to no avail. Finally, we arrived at the shelter and went down the steps into the deep, narrow tunnel where two parallel rows of benches lined the grey cement walls.

Auntie Superintendent and her respectable friends sat down next to the people already perched on the narrow benches, all of them wrapped in blankets against the cold. Our small group – Mária, Aunt Marika, Nagyi and I – took our places at the back of the shelter. It was wiser not to expose ourselves too much to the scrutiny of strangers in case something in our appearance, speech or behaviour betrayed our ethnic origin. We sat there, separate from the others, listening to the muted sounds of battle all day long. Then, under the cover of darkness, we crept back to our insecure shelter, the mattresses on the sagging springs of ancient iron bedsteads, and ate something that passed for an evening meal.

In the morning, I was adamant. I wept and screamed and refused to budge. My grandmother, whose nerves by now had been stretched to the limit, gave me one of her withering looks, threw down the pile of blankets she had collected for the journey and muttered angrily, "All right, Miss Hysteria. I'd rather die than listen to this. We will stay. Just stop!"

The epithet, Miss Hysteria, was usually counterproductive and only made me turn up the volume of my protestations. This time, I stopped crying immediately and allowed Nagyi to savour her verbal victory. To my relief, the treacherous trip to the dismal bomb shelter was cancelled. We spent another day in our cellar, listening to the escalating sounds of combat, to my perverse relief.

In the evening, when the other tenants returned, they had terrible news. A bomb had pierced the cement casing of the shelter, thought to be impregnable. It had made a huge hole in the back, where we had sat the previous day. Surely, we would have chosen the same place again. Once more, we had narrowly escaped.

One day in February the sun slanted through gaps in the oilskin covering the glassless panes of the basement door. Everything was quiet. We knew that soon Soviets would be coming to "liberate" us, in addition to possibly "liberating" us of some of the few belongings we still possessed. Mária and my aunt hid, assuming that the rumours about the soldiers' behaviour toward young women were true.

And then, he was there. A short, dark-haired man in a Soviet uniform with rows of shiny medals suspended from bright ribbons on his chest. He had a kind, intelligent face. We had learned a few words of Russian in anticipation and I called out a brave hello –

"Zdrastvuitye." To our surprise, he did not answer in Russian, but instead asked, "Parlez-vous français?" (Do you speak French?). This was Nagyi's moment. In her inimitable Hungarian schoolgirl French, she answered yes, "Vooi," gradually recovering her air of respectability as she translated for the inhabitants of the cellar the news that the Germans had finally capitulated. The war was over in Budapest.

Afterward

Only after the Battle of Budapest was over, and the city had been officially liberated by the Soviets, did Mária and Aunt Marika dare to leave their hiding places. It was February 1945 and all that was left of the apartment we had abandoned on Christmas Eve was a pile of rubble. There was no time to regret lost things. We were alive. I remember walking with Mária, crossing the Danube over one of the temporary bridges. The once-graceful arches spanning the river were tangles of twisted metal on broken stone pillars. On our way, we saw houses razed to the ground or cut in half, grotesque cross-sections with pieces of furniture and wall paintings that appeared to hang in mid-air. In some, only parts of floor were still intact, indecently exposed to view.

When we reached the elegant building where my mother's family had once lived, we saw that the stucco outer walls were pockmarked with bullet holes. The apartment, however, was miraculously untouched by the war. Mária left me with Nagyi and Aunt Marika. Life would begin to assume some normalcy. I didn't belong to her anymore.

Mária, too, was ready to begin another life. Our parting was painful for both of us, but she promised to take me on an outing every Sunday. This was our secret, our weekly visit to mass. Nobody in my family would have approved of my continued religious zeal. To the world, I was once more Judit Grünfeld but now my secret identity was Ilona Papp, who loved to go to church.

My family's apartment was located in one of the better neighbourhoods of Pest (in Lipótváros, the Fifth District), behind the parliament and the boardwalk along the Danube. It was a dark and sombre place. My grandmother, dressed in her usual black, and Aunt Marika, clothed tastefully in muted shades, were barely distinguishable from the few pieces of heavy, cheerless, dark-wood furniture upholstered in grey. I felt alone in the oppressive silence, where the women never ceased to listen for voices of those who were not there.

My stay with Nagyi and Aunt Marika came to an end when my father's family asserted their patriarchal claim. The nebulous victory belonged to the Grünfelds, who decided that the home of my aunt Elza, my father's elder sister, would be the right place for me. Elza had grandchildren my age living with her. I had mixed feelings about this change: apprehensive about moving in with a family of near-strangers, relieved that I would be escaping my grandmother's stern and hygienic custody, and slightly guilty at feeling pleased.

Before the war, my parents and I had lived on the third floor of my father's family's three-storey apartment building located in a less-fashionable part of the city. His parents, two brothers and sister, Elza, lived in the house too, but were much less familiar to me than my mother's relations. After her marriage, my mother had still maintained her allegiance to the elegant Fifth District where she had grown up, and to her family of four sisters and one brother. It was a true matriarchy, ruled by my widowed grandmother. She tolerated her sons-in-law affectionately, but they were mere bit players during the pre-war Sunday night ritual dinners filled with female chatter. At the end of these evenings my two cousins and I would stand chafing in the vestibule for what seemed like hours; the sisters were always reluctant to terminate an ongoing conversation or close the door behind them to leave and go their separate ways.

My entry into Aunt Elza's crowded and somewhat chaotic apartment was a new experience. During the weeks I spent there, I had more fun than ever before in my life. Uncle Desző, a heavy-set, grey-haired, nervous man, had quirky ways and was always preoccupied with some new business venture. His post-war enterprise involved a large quantity of tinned goods with bright labels and preserves – mostly pickles of various sizes and hues. Insomnia must have driven him to move the mountains of tins and jars from place to place because early each morning the pickles were relocated from one wall to another of what had been their living room before the war. His wife, Aunt Elza, was short and plump and as funny and loving as Mária. She prepared delicious meals: chicken soup with lots of dumplings, veal or chicken paprikash, Hungarian-style overcooked vegetables swimming in sauce and rich pastries. Her hot cocoa was thick enough to eat with a spoon. All this, thanks to Uncle Desző's connections in the black market.

Aunt Elza told stories and listened to ours – those of my cousins, Tomi and Peter, and mine. She was our caretaker and confidante more than their mother, whom I called Aunt Hilda, an attractive woman with dyed-blond hair and high heels. Hilda was waiting for her husband, Uncle Géza (Géza bácsi), who had not come back from the forced labour battalions, the *munkaszolgálat*, to which Hungarian Jews had been assigned. He never did return.

My cousins were only slightly older than me, but much wiser in the ways of the world and childhood fun. They introduced me to pillow-fights on the day we were given our first typhoid vaccine. As soon as the door closed behind the adults, we romped from their beds to my sofa, ignoring all the warnings about the consequences of this exercise. We only stopped when, as predicted, our arms and shoulders began to throb and ache and fever hammers echoed in our heads. Tomi and Peter were happy to have a girl to join their games. They taught me to play cards, a repertory of bad words, and entertained me with music. Tomi, who later became a professional musician, was already good at playing the accordion. They also pursued an interest in anatomy, studying the female body from their resident live model.

Nobody mentioned the words "concentration camp" or "death." My cousins' father and uncles had been "taken away," others were "dragged away," and they were eventually simply "lost." Only one of Aunt Elza's three sons, Uncle Paul (Pali bácsi), was found making his way from Auschwitz, mostly on foot. I overheard rumours about what had happened to Jews there, but I don't think any of these were real to me until I saw them in photographs and films many years later. Uncle Paul didn't tell anyone about his experiences, but he never really seemed to have escaped. Failure and depression haunted him until, once more in exile from Communist Hungary in 1948, he committed suicide in a refugee camp in Vienna.

Other members of the family slowly drifted back from hiding, from the countryside, from forced labour contingents, and from places as far away as Romania or the Soviet Union. They were more ready to go on with their lives. On the first floor, my grandfather moved in with Uncle Max (Misi bácsi) and Aunt Lula (Lula néni). My grandmother, whom we called Katrin mama, had died from a shrapnel wound in the windowless bathroom of the apartment – the improvised shelter where they had hidden. Years later, I saw a brownish stain on a spare pillow in the house and refused to use it, imagining that this was the one on which she had lain slowly bleeding to death on the tile floor.

Aunt Helen (Ilonka néni) returned to her second-floor apartment. She had survived as a maid in a Budapest hospital, using false documents from a neighbour in the village where she was born. Her two tall sons joined her and tried to continue their school lives, playing ping-pong and soccer and socializing with girls.

My father's family had been successful in business. They bought and sold wine, beer and other forms of alcohol. I loved the cool air and the musty smell of wine barrels that escaped from the cellar under our house. There was a wagon used for transportation, pulled by Bubi, a sturdy, placid, brown workhorse. He stood for hours in front of the house, immobile except for munching inside the feed bag attached to his ears and flicking his tail to whisk away the flies. He exuded a special aroma that consisted of fodder, straw and manure.

Across the street was a retail outlet – and that's where the trouble that eventually propelled me to the first floor began. Unsupervised in Aunt Elza's easygoing ground-floor apartment, I often wandered alone to watch Bubi and talk to the workers who rolled and hoisted the heavy barrels on to the wagon. Eventually, I got into the habit of paying a daily visit to the pub where workers dropped in for a glass of wine, a shot of powerful Hungarian fruit brandy or a mug of frothy beer. The bartender knew my fondness for the white foam and usually offered me a *piccolo*, a small glass of blond beer with lots of bubbles.

When news of my drinking habits reached the ears of my proper Ilonka néni, a family council was quickly summoned. Her apartment, often full of adolescent boys, was not considered an appropriate substitute for the lax morals of my Aunt Elza's home. It was decided that I should move to the first floor to join my grandfather and Uncle Max and Aunt Lula, who were childless.

Uncle Max was kind but gruff and spent most of his time in the cellar and the office behind the pub, rebuilding the family enterprise. Aunt Lula, a buxom lady particularly fond of tight, purple wool dresses, was a businesswoman too, although her ventures did not always result in material gain. She was away from the apartment much of the time and I was alone again. Solitude drove me to write poetry. In a leather-bound volume, years later, I found one of my poems addressed to a migrating bird. I sympathized with him for having to leave his homeland, but envied him because he was not motherless, like me. I must have begun to miss my parents.

Then, one day in the fall of 1945, when the chestnuts of Fasor were ripe for picking, they were there. I don't remember feeling joy, but more a sense of strangeness and embarrassment. Could I be right? My parents seemed smaller than I had remembered them. I looked at the small, thin, nervous lady whom I would call Anyu (Mother) again and remembered another Anyu from before.

~

I have a memory of my mother and me before the war. We are sitting together sewing, or rather mending socks. The Hungarian word is *stoppolni*, to mend the holes and make the socks whole, to save them from going to waste. I am five or six years old. It's a winter afternoon and already dark. My mother has turned on the recessed lamps around the mirror of her dressing table to give us some light. Frosted glass shells enclose the bulbs, their muted glow reflected twice – in the oval mirror and in faint pinpoints along the black glass dressing table. I love sitting at my mother's feet on a blue velvet stool, and I especially love the musty fragrance of the sprinkles of powder she dabs on her cheeks. We are mending socks and our reflections are, too. Hers is weaving a tight mesh, in and out, over and under, with her fine needle and soft, thin thread. She has inserted a shiny mushroom-shaped piece of wood into the opening of the hole to keep the fabric taut, matching the web of thread to the sock until it is whole once more. I have a miniature mushroom and a discarded sock to stitch with my large, wide-eyed needle. I cut a long thread with my mother's scissors, which resembles the beak of a bird.

Now I am eight years old. The sun shines brightly. My mother and I are once more mending socks. We are sitting at the window of Aunt Elza's apartment. Instead of a dressing-room mirror, my mother's room has a huge hole in the wall left by a cannon shell. The woman who had lived there while we were away drew pictures of naked women, entertained Soviet soldiers and kept chickens in the room. She is no longer there. My mother's room is being repaired. My mother is teaching me how to mend socks: over and under. I keep forgetting to always skip one thread. I'm supposed to be happy that my mother is back. I didn't recognize her face when she kissed me for the first time after her return. Sundays I'm not allowed to go to church with Mária anymore.

~

Now that my mother, father and I were together again, we worked at rebuilding our damaged apartment and our severed relationship. My father, hoping to replace my church outings with Mária, enrolled me in a Zionist youth movement. My mother also thought I'd like to join the Girl Guides with my cousin Zsuzsa. In order to be accepted as a member I had to learn to tie intricate knots, which I could never master, and could never quite understand why I should. I didn't bother to join. At their Sunday meetings, the teenaged Zionist members spent most of the time rehearsing shadow plays behind suspended sheets and re-enacting battles between settlers, Arabs and British soldiers; we, the young ones, had to stand and recite incomprehensible verses from yellowed typed papers. I managed to miss Sunday meetings as often as I could.

It was only as an adult that I heard the French description of a certain type of person as *déraciné*. The literal translation is "rootless," but I think it refers rather to someone able to transcend the need for permanent roots, as I think I have.

Dragons and Departures

Memory plays strange games of hide-and-seek. One day, during a brief stay in Sweden in 2002, I saw the familiar Pfaff symbol in the window of a shop selling sewing machines. It was a splayed lizard, in an iron net, a giant spiderweb. I didn't pay much attention to it until it resurfaced in a dream that night. The last time I had seen the lizard was on the wheel of a pedal-operated sewing machine in post-war Budapest. It had been an inheritance from my father's mother, but since my mother never used the mechanical contraption, it stayed behind with most of our belongings when we left Hungary to create a new life in Canada a few years later.

In Montreal, my mother did start to sew, but on a small electric sewing machine purchased after my father had tried and failed at many business enterprises. She began to sew her own clothes, some of mine, and then tried to create sets of beaded satin collars and cuffs for sale in the elegant boutiques of the city. I hated the sound of the sewing machine whirring late into the night. My mother produced dresses and skirts for us with the best of intentions, following the instructions of the flimsy paper patterns meticulously. Somehow, we never ended up looking like the attractive well-dressed women and girls on the pattern envelopes from Vogue or McCall's.

The carefully packed boxes lined with tissue paper piled ever higher on my mother's dresser in the cramped, narrow room. Nobody seemed to need satin trimmings on sweaters and suits.

I eventually inherited my mother's electric sewing machine, a solid Singer in a black leather case, and hid it in the depths of a closet. No need to conjure up memories of satin and cotton, the grey felt skirt with poodles or the pale blue backless sundress with the modest bolero jacket. When a friend asked to borrow it and failed to return it, I was relieved. I preferred to buy my clothes and I had no talent for, or interest in, sewing. I managed to banish all thoughts of sewing machines – until the day I saw the familiar lizard-dragon in the Stockholm shop window.

That night, in my dream, I kept repeating the word "Pfaff." I was somewhat puzzled. Suddenly, an androgynous voice bellowed the message that "Pfaff" was the name of a town in Sweden; if I could uncover the memory hidden there, my mother would find forgiveness. I woke in the middle of that night, continuing to toss in semi-sleep, searching for the meaning of "Pfaff." I realized that there was no town by this name and that nobody in my family had ever been to Sweden before me. Why did my mother need to be forgiven? It was only in the morning that the memory of "Pfaff" returned.

Before the war, my grandmother's old sewing machine had stood silent and unused, covered by a large lace doily for years in my grandparents' apartment. After the war, it moved into our apartment, to an unused room that several times a year became the domain of the woman I called Aunt Klári (Klári néni), a drab, poverty-stricken and history-worn Jewish woman, a seamstress with thick glasses that sheltered and magnified her protruding eyes. She worked in our house for a few days each season hemming sheets, repairing linen and making dresses and skirts, often for me. I remember one in particular: a plaid skirt with wide shoulder straps. The pattern of horizontal and vertical lines in oranges and yellows had no connection with any traditional Scottish tartan, and its style was not in sync with any fashion of any particular place or time. As I grew, this outfit grew with me. Aunt Klári always left plenty of material in the seams. When I first wore it, the shoulder straps lay flat against my chest; but before finally disappearing from my wardrobe and my life, my newly developing breasts had begun to strain against them suggestively.

That was in Grade 6, when I almost never went to school because we were about to defect from Hungary. It was all very secretive, involving visas and passports and deals with authorities. On the few occasions when I did go to school, I already felt like an alien among my classmates. I wore the familiar outfit to class on one of my rare ventures to school. My friend Ági, a small girl with no feminine attributes, passed me in the aisle, looked me up and down as though I were a stranger and, pointing in the direction of the taut plaid, made a lewd gesture indicating bulging protrusions.

I felt as if I had already become a defector in every sense – I was now on the side of the adults and no longer in the "group." I envied Ági, her flat chest, her freckles and curly, red hair, her tiny, cold apartment in a crumbling building. My well-heated apartment with its carpets and modern furniture and my grandmother in the fashionable Fifth District of Budapest had all set me apart. Now I had to suffer the betrayal of the plaid shoulder straps.

Aunt Klári made "Pfaff," the splayed lizard, turn faster and faster on the wheel at the side of the sewing machine as she moved it with her pudgy hands. Her feet pumped the pedals up and down, full of energy in spite of the swollen ankles above the bulging laced shoes. The needle raced in and out of the cloth, the seamstress's eyes behind the convex spectacles never straying, following the progress of cotton, wool, silk and the new synthetic material we called by one generic name – nylon. This was the stuff that halted the insistent needle time and again, bunching up the smoothly flowing cloth. Aunt Klári would then stop the lizard and open the secret compartment under the metal cover where small bobbins of thread duplicated the progress of the large spools turning dizzily on stakes driven into the massive body of the machine. After some brief manipulation above and below, she untangled the knots, smoothing out the fabric so that the lizard could resume its dizzying whirl – a black, steamless locomotive with no visible tracks.

"Pfaff." What did this innocuous, metal reptile have to do with my mother and forgiveness? In my mind, "Pfaff" had become "Fafner"... the name of the dragon in German myths, the "dragon" that had tried to annihilate us all – Aunt Klári, my mother and me. It had blown away my grandmother, Katrin mama, leaving behind only her sewing machine with the lizard on the wheel. Its fiery breath had devoured my tiny grandmother as she crouched in the windowless bathroom to escape the bombs and cannon shells. Dragon-blood-filled young men searching for hidden Jews. Pouf! The shrapnel that had pierced the wall and the pulsing vein under my grandmother's transparent temple. Such rivers of blood!

Pouf! Objects disappeared. Pouf! Our comfortable lives! Our apartment, where a cannonball had opened a gash the size of a dragon's egg in my mother's room, allowing the rain and snow to soak the dusky blue-white dotted velvet of her sofa and peel the veneer of cherrywood from the dressing table under the smashed mirror.

Pouf! The holidays in the Mátra Mountains and by Lake Balaton. The dinners with my aunts, uncles and cousins around the dining room table in the elegant apartment in the grey stucco building behind the parliament near the river drive.

Pouf! My mother's warm hand holding mine, walking under the flowering trees toward the park. Is that the forgiveness my mother found in Sweden? Did I forgive her for taking that walk with me to the convent, abandoning me so that I would remain alive?

~

I spent my last summer in Hungary, the summer of 1948, on Lake Balaton in a summer camp run by my music teacher, Uncle Gyuri (Gyuri bácsi). It was organized for his piano students and any other children willing to pay. In post–World War II Hungary, not many parents could afford even the modest rates Uncle Gyuri charged and those who could preferred to hide and hoard their assets in preparation for imminent departure from Communist Hungary. My father's family, who had always been in business, were considered "class enemies." Tolerance was only temporary for our bourgeois lifestyle – the large apartment, the cellar where my father's family kept the large barrels of wine to be sold wholesale and the pub that served beer and wine by the glass to the neighbourhood workers.

By 1948, it had become obvious that only tenuous threads attached us to the city of Budapest and the country of Hungary. There was talk of passports and visas; the word *disszidált*, which loosely translates as "defected" was applied to the members of our family who no longer showed up for Sunday dinner at my grandmother's. Thanks to his two elder brothers' connections, my father had managed to leave Soviet-occupied Hungary that spring, the last year that Hungarian passports were still issued for "tourists." They were valid for only three months at a time. My mother and I were to follow him in the fall.

I remember the spring day in 1948 after my father had left when two men in belted raincoats, like secret agents in the movies, came to the door of our apartment in Budapest. They were Államvédelmi Osztálya (ávo) officers, the Hungarian equivalents of the Soviet secret police. Suspicion had been aroused when my father, a capitalist "class alien," had suddenly taken a train from Budapest to Vienna. He was already waiting for us to join him there, before the Hungarian border to Austria closed completely.

The men in belted raincoats entered our apartment, looked about suspiciously, and told my mother to follow them.

"Where?" she asked, knowing that the answer would be Andrássy Street 66, their infamous headquarters, a white-washed building on one of the most elegant streets of Budapest. Bright red geraniums in the window boxes outside the grated windows of the prison cells deceived no one.

"Give me some time to let the babysitter know about my daughter's outing tomorrow. She needs to pack a picnic lunch."

They must have been pleased to find such an unemotional victim and waited willingly while she gave instructions about sandwiches, apples and juice to Erzsi, our maid, reassuring us that she would be back soon.

"Who did your husband spy for?" the interrogator wanted to know at headquarters. "I could deny the accusation in all honesty," my mother laughingly recalled later. Who would engage my absent-minded bookworm of a father, inefficient even as a businessman, as a spy? Hours of interrogation came up with nothing. She was released from prison after a few days, unharmed.

My mother tried to maintain an aura of normalcy in our lives, which is why I was sent to Uncle Gyuri's camp on the southern bank of Lake Balaton. This was supposed to be a brief interlude of stability before my world would come apart again. Uncle Gyuri and Aunt Klári, his wife, rented a cottage every summer for the motley, ill-assorted dozen or so campers ranging from five to twelve years old. The older kids – my friend Éva, who was twelve, Ági, who must have been sixteen and I – helped out with the little ones. I was eleven years old and had just finished fifth grade, considered the first year of secondary school, or *gimnázium*, where I was a good student. I was better at history and creative writing than math, but I had a particular penchant for poetry. I was a romantic preteen.

That summer I fell in love with a boy named George. He was short and swarthy, the owner of a blue rubber kayak his parents had brought to camp in their cream-coloured convertible in defiance of the anti-capitalist politics of the day. Although we were both eleven years old, I towered a head above him, but that didn't deter me from entertaining romantic fantasies. He was funny, had wavy black hair and suggestive, large brown eyes. One morning we made a date for our first kiss.

"See you after lunch! Put your blanket under the acacia tree," George whispered with a meaningful wink after breakfast, before disappearing on a frog-hunting expedition in the bulrushes by the lake. There were few organized activities except for the after-lunch siesta. It was the perfect time to engage in touching hands, exchanging notes or simply dreaming of contact, listening to the whispering of the trees above our heads. Acacia leaves are clustered in small paired or odd-numbered leaves attached to a thin common stem. We used these, like daisy petals, to predict our future. Pulling them off one by one we mumbled, "He loves me, loves me not, to the altar, till the grave" – a most conventional view of love.

My hormones were buzzing louder than the annoying clouds of mosquitoes by the lake as I smoothed my grey flannel blanket over the lumpy grass at the root of the tree. As camouflage, I brought along a book, *The Prisoners of God*, the story of a Hungarian princess who threatened to cut off her nose if her royal father insisted on her marriage to a foreign prince and didn't let her become a nun. She wanted to be the bride of Christ. Not me! I had outgrown my devout dreams. I was going to kiss George this afternoon.

The blankets of all the campers spread out in random patterns. The little children had fluffy pastel-coloured ones on which they managed to nap, a deep sleep that eluded us seniors. I looked around in anticipation. There was Éva's red-and-green English-plaid blanket with soft fringes by the bushes at the edge of the field. And next to her... I couldn't believe my eyes! There was George's yellow imported American quilt, with its pattern of cowboys lassoing invisible prey. They giggled happily together as though sharing a terrific joke: ME! Under the acacia, all alone.

That afternoon I borrowed the kayak George's parents had brought to camp and paddled toward the middle of the lake, gliding and dipping, dipping and gliding, tears streaming down my face. I reached out with my tongue to lick the salty drops, proof of my deep sorrow, contemplating the pained faces at camp when news of my drowning would reach them. My disappearance and the overturned kayak on the water would surely be connected. But then the laughter of Éva and George seemed to reverberate against the cliffs of Tihany above the lake famous for its echo effects. I realized that they would only be pleased.

I pushed the long paddle into the water, turning the prow toward the camp, and, dipping and gliding, gliding and dipping, returned in sullen silence. Nobody had missed me. I skipped dinner and crawled under the covers, pretending to be asleep when Éva came in that night. The next day, I unloaded my troubles on Ági, who was now my best friend, until an urgent call from my mother summoned me back to Budapest. She didn't tell me on the phone, but I knew. We were leaving for the West.

That was my last Hungarian summer.

Escape

The wheels of the train creaked rhythmically, lurching past the stubbled, harvested fields of the many cooperative farms. Past the railway platforms of villages where blank-faced peasants gazed with longing at the letters on the side of the wagons: "Budapest-Vienna." The words spelled E-S-C-A-P-E. We were lucky, or almost. The border was still to come.

I sat in the railway carriage, demure in my short, navy, pleated skirt. Rays of the autumn sun fell on the book in my lap. I had brought along *The Prisoners of God*, the bulky volume I had reread several times since the summer. Suddenly, a familiar sensation of fear descended into the pit of my stomach. What if the title betrayed me to the border guard? After all, we had been told that the only prisons in Hungary at the time were for "class enemies" and there was no God anymore. The Holy Trinity had been replaced by the triumvirate of Marx, Lenin and Stalin and their disciple, the Hungarian Communist dictator, Mátyás Rákosi.

The red, white and green arm of the barrier was raised to let the train pass and then lowered again behind it. The uniformed agent glanced carefully at my face, but not at the volume in my lap, as he handled the crisp, green, bound passport my mother had procured for us at quite a price, trading our apartment and many of our valuables for the document. There were stories attached to our departure, first to my father's, then ours – stories I would hear only years later. I felt safe at last as the train sang a new song, a German refrain on the Austrian tracks.

I opened my book and a bit of paper fell out, the last fragment of a postcard from Éva. Before I had torn the card into shreds, the message, in her even, flowing script had read:

"Dear Jutka, Sorry you had to leave camp early. George and I are having so much fun. We both miss you. Kisses, Éva."

Under the signature was a postscript with a decidedly unloving epithet in a scrawl I recognized as George's from the many secret notes passed to me under the acacia tree before the mysteriously aborted kissing appointment not so long ago.

~

The only pictures of Vienna I had in my mind were based on old prints and illustrations: castles, like wedding cakes in pastel shades, ladies with crinolines, in silks, with powdered hair, fans in hand. Reality was a colourless, war-battered city. The cloudy days in our cramped, unheated rented room were unending. Heating was expensive, our landlady thought, and besides, there were too many refugees in the city already, why make them feel at home? We swathed ourselves in layers of sweaters to keep warm, waiting for our Canadian visas.

The Hungarian passports my mother had procured for us in Budapest in exchange for our apartment were about to expire in December 1948. In order to prevent deportation by the Soviets, who controlled the part of Austria surrounding Vienna (a city divided and administered by the four Allies: United States, Great Britain, France and the USSR), my mother and I took the train out of the city on the eve of St. Nicholas Day, December 6. Heading for Salzburg, a more congenial, American-controlled town in the Alps, we settled into our berths in the sleeping compartment of the rickety train. My mother put my shoes on the table under the window and in them she put the traditional gilded branches hung with candies that St. Nicholas brings to all good children on that night. It was a ruse to soften the hearts of the Soviet soldiers who would come to check our documents. They were known to be partial to children.

I was already a fairly tall eleven-year-old, so I snuggled under the covers, pulling up my long legs to seem diminutive. My heart beat furiously when the Soviet soldier entered our compartment and asked for our passports. Would we be allowed to leave the Soviet sector and glide into freedom in American-controlled Austria? Or would we be deported back to Communist Hungary? I closed my eyes while the uniformed guard checked our passports. He must have pointed to the gilded branches in the window indicating the presence of a child, because I heard a friendly, male voice with a distinctly Russian accent ask my mother in German, "Kind?" (A child?) Me. My mother answered in the affirmative. The compartment door clicked shut. The next morning I woke up, free, in Salzburg.

~

Salzburg had been untouched by the war. Although the sky was still grey and the weather not any friendlier than in Vienna, our lives had become much brighter. We moved into a large room in a fine hotel called Roter Krebs (Red Crab) at the exorbitant sum of one dollar per day; for another dollar we ate our lunch in the Gabler Hotel, where a uniformed waiter poured golden chicken soup with dumplings from a silver server into our soup bowls. As long as my mother and I were by ourselves we lived this luxurious existence, going to the local theatre to see operettas and puppet shows on the weekend. During the week, I went to a girls' high school (in German, a *Gymnasium*) where, in spite of my meagre language skills, I managed to learn German poetry and even physics, copying the notebook of my new best friend, Monika.

These happy days came to an end when my father joined us. We had looked forward to his arrival from Vienna, but I was disappointed when he enjoined us to stop wasting our limited foreign capital and abandon our favourite restaurant. He instead procured an electric hot plate, on which my mother heated the contents of cans my father bought at the local army PX (the Post Exchange that was set up by the American military for soldiers to buy goods). At night my father and I went on missions to "lose" the empty tins in the trash cans of exotic locations, like the cathedral square where the church bells played the bird-catcher's tune from Mozart's *The Magic Flute*. We weren't explicitly told not to cook in our room, but we worried that once the management saw the evidence of our culinary explorations, we would be asked to leave. Not that the odour of tinned potatoes and corned beef cooked in paprika sauce was easy to camouflage. It was embarrassingly obvious to me as I climbed the carpeted stairs on my return from school. So my father and I "disappeared" the evidence after darkness fell.

At the end of March 1949 our visas finally arrived. We were now officially "stateless" immigrants and had the right to arrange passage to Canada from the German port of Bremen. As DPs (displaced persons) we had to say goodbye to our current lifestyle. Even our dinners of tinned potatoes, Spam and canned peaches were a step above the food at the barracks of the DP camp on the outskirts of Bremen, where we were housed. Before our ship departed, our bodies and our documents were screened, we were inoculated against any possible disease we might be bringing to Canada and finally allowed to embark on the SS *Scythia*, the ocean liner that would take us to our new country.

It was during the days of our temporary incarceration in the DP camp that we met Mr. and Mrs. N, a Romanian couple with a compatible middle-class background, unlike many of the other prospective immigrants. Mrs. N was tiny and dark, shorter than I. She often wore an ivory silk blouse under a bright green woollen suit jacket made of a material softer to the touch than most of the post-war fabrics that made up our new clothes. She hugged me a lot, kissing me on both cheeks whenever we met, leaving behind a scent of a delicious perfume. She was from Bucharest, where the women, according to my mother, were almost as elegant as the Parisian ladies. I think my mother may have said these words in a tone of derision, for Mrs. N wore a little too much makeup and teetered on thin, high heels. My mother only wore lipstick and pale face powder on her cheeks, and always wore sensible shoes. I adored Mrs. N immediately, relished the French she spoke to my parents that bubbled and gurgled in the back of her throat, her lips in a perpetual pucker as though she was sucking on lemon drops, or was about to blow a kiss.

Mr. N spoke German with us, with an accent that I recognized as very different from my father's casual Austrian pronunciation or from my mother's school German. After four months in Austrian schools, the German I had spoken with my nannies until I was three years old had returned and I could now hold long, meaningful conversations on a variety of topics.

Mr. N was a burly man and wore dark woollen suits with ties. His reddish thinning hair had a grey tinge belying the smooth cheeks, the youthful smile. The humorous twinkle in his eyes, when focused on me, seemed to imply that I was a person, not just "the child."

My parents were grateful that he took me for walks and entertained me for hours during the long afternoons of coffee and endless conversations about visas, ration cards and other refugees. If my parents had only known the topics of our conversations! Mr. N educated me about "love." He described with precision how to kiss in different ways, and related in detail the role of the man and the woman when making love.

"How long does it take?" I asked.

"That all depends, could be minutes, could be hours."

"What does it depend on?" I wanted to know.

I began to wonder whether, given an appropriate time and place, we would progress to demonstrations. Had I forgotten about Mrs. N?

At this stage of my apprenticeship, we prepared to leave. O Canada! Glorious and free! Our families travelled together to the German port of Bremen to finally board the SS *Scythia* for Halifax. Mr. N and my father bedded down in the dormitories in the hold of the ship, where hundreds of male refugees vomited, snored and dreamed of a new world, while my mother, Mrs. N and I enjoyed the luxury of a cabin closer to the deck. This time I was happy to be considered a child. The cabins usually housed twelve people, but my being a child entitled us to a cabin with four bunk beds for only eight passengers. Mrs. N must have claimed ill health with the addition of some welcome American dollars to enjoy an upper berth in such relative luxury.

Mr. N and I did not continue our intimate walks. My mind was not on finding a place for lovers' trysts. I spent most of the trip leaning over the railing, with the wind trailing away the few bits of food my mother had managed to coax me to eat. One day, while trying to balance on the toilet seat, a precarious perch that kept shifting with the waves, drops of blood hit the turbulent waters in the bowl under me. "The joy and glory of becoming a woman" Mr. N promised had arrived, but there was only pain in my abdomen and nausea.

"Mother! I need some cotton wool!" was the only way I could find to share the embarrassing news. It was April, my birthday month. I had turned twelve by the time the shores of Canada were in sight.

～

One warm summer day after our arrival in Montreal, Mr. and Mrs. N came for coffee and cake to our new apartment off Cote-des-Neiges Road. Mrs. N was quieter than she had been in Europe and Mr. N seemed to have aged during the previous few months. His woollen suit was tight and the buttons of his jacket strained at the waist. It was not quite the right outfit for the season. Did I smell perspiration? His hair also seemed to have thinned.

I avoided him by keeping myself busy with cups and saucers and platters of sweets, but in spite of all my efforts to remain at a distance from him, we met as I passed through the doorway of the living room on some errand from the kitchen. I tried to make myself very small. Not small enough. Mr. N reached out with his hand – I had not noticed before how stubby his fingers were – and I drew in my breath. He touched my breasts, taut under the blouse of white silk, transparent, in spite of a lace camisole.

"You're really getting bigger, aren't you?"

No answer was required. I squirmed and ducked to escape; I didn't leave my perch at the edge of a high-backed chair at a safe distance from Mr. N until all the guests had gone.

Later, I told my parents of Mr. N's unwelcome gesture. I skilfully omitted the consensual conversations we had in Bremen during the past winter, which seemed like a very long time ago. My parents never invited Mr. or Mrs. N over again.

New Adjustments

Soon after our arrival, my father took me to the nearby Iona Avenue School to register. The principal's name was Mr. Gulliver – the sign on his office door said so. Mr. Gulliver sat behind a massive oak desk under a picture of King George in uniform. My father handed him my Hungarian report card, which had been translated into English, stamped and signed to prove that it was a genuine record of my marks in fifth grade, my last school year in Budapest. Attached was a brief letter in German: no grades, just official seals and signatures testifying that I had attended a boarding school in Vienna for one month and a *Gymnasium* in Salzburg for three.

Mr. Gulliver stood up, reaching for a cane that leaned against his desk. He was a stocky man with powerful shoulders and a lame foot. He grasped the cane and hobbled closer, glancing from the papers to me. Strict, I thought, but not mean.

"You are a tall girl," he observed. At just over 165 centimetres, I already towered above my father and was almost the same height as the principal. "This is a good report card," Mr. Gulliver added. I had only taken a few English lessons in Salzburg, not enough to understand his comments, but my father, who prided himself on speaking at least ten languages, four of them with native-like proficiency (if not with the local accent), translated for me.

"Please, please," I begged silently. "Don't put me back a grade." My memories of the humiliating months spent with puny ten-year-olds in the dormitory of the Viennese boarding school were still fresh.

"I will take you to meet your classmates in Grade 6." One, two, three, four, five, SIX. Thank God! I followed Mr. Gulliver's uneven steps out of the office, along the long corridors lined with camouflage-green metal lockers, and up the deserted stairs to the door of the classroom.

The teacher who answered the knock was grey: she had grey hair, wore a grey suit and had a distinctly cheerless look on her wrinkled face, which was suddenly transformed by a toothy smile when she saw the principal at her door. Four rows of students snapped to attention and chorused, "Good morning, Mr. Gulliver." They stood up and twenty-four wooden seats hit the backs of their desks. At the teacher's command, there was another clatter of metal and wood. The seats snapped back down. Twenty-four pairs of eyes scrutinized me as I stood in front like an exotic insect impaled on the blackboard.

Mr. Gulliver introduced me to my new teacher, Miss Brown, who bestowed upon me a shadow of the smile with which she had welcomed the principal. She turned to the class referring to me by my new, Canadian name, Judy. In Hungarian, J is pronounced like a Y – a soft, liquid sound. "Judy" was harsh, unfamiliar. It was not the biblical "Judit," nor the diminutive, "Jutka." The other words she used meant nothing to me. I understood nothing.

I thought about the brown and green desks of my old classroom in Budapest, where two girls shared a bench. My best friend, Veronika, always sat next to me. The seats there did not spring up with a racket, and the familiar ham-shaped map of Hungary dominated the wall above the blackboard. No maps here, but another photograph of the king, who seemed to be looking down with a smile at the flag by the window. It was a red flag with a small Union Jack in the corner. The Hungarian red, white and green flag had a five-pointed red Soviet star in the middle.

Posters of wild landscapes decorated the walls. A single tree, twisting in the wind over stormy waves and another of a forest that seemed to be on fire with its orange and scarlet leaves. The scenes were as alien to me as the words pouring out of the teacher's mouth. In Hungary, I could locate the rivers of the country, the Danube and the Tisza, and all the counties with their capitals on the classroom wall map. I could recite the poems of the famous Hungarian poets, Petőfi and Arany and Endre Ady. But what was the use? Nobody here would understand or care.

"Judy!" The name called was mine. Miss Brown's voice jarred me to attention. She motioned me to an empty desk in the second row. I obeyed. My brown, laced shoes were like weights, dragging my feet across the floor. I sat down. I tried to smile at the boy in the next row whose curious eyes followed my every movement. He turned away and, without looking at me again, picked up his pen, dipped it into the inkwell on his desk, wiped the excess moisture off the nib and began to write. The paper in front of him was filling up with twin columns, in the same spidery hand I saw on the board as the teacher dictated words, one by one, to the army of pens marching along lined papers.

At last, I recognized one word. It sounded like *kálcium*. In my old school we had just begun to study chemistry. I had been looking forward to the lessons until that October day when my mother told me, "Pack quickly! We finally received our passports. Now we can leave the country." She seemed jubilant. I was not so sure.

"When are we coming back?" I had asked her.

"Maybe in a few years, if…" If what? If what? I thought, but I knew better than to harass my agitated mother with my questions.

Now I was in Canada, an ocean away from everything I knew and from everyone who knew me. The teacher continued to pronounce the words. I didn't even have a paper in front of me like all the other students.

Set into the desk was an inkwell with a hinged metal lid. I checked. No ink inside.

Another word I recognized: *oksigén*. What you need to breathe. I held my breath and lifted the metal lid of the inkwell set in a circular hole in my desk… slowly, with one finger. No danger. It was just an empty container. I let the lid down very, very carefully. Not a sound. Good!

I heard a new word that was like *hidrogén*. H_2O – I had learned this was water. I was thirsty but I realized that I didn't know how to ask to be excused to get a drink.

I repeated the inkwell-lid manoeuvre again and again. I was really getting very good at raising and lowering the metal top, until a sudden unintentional pressure of my finger sent the whole inkwell soaring into the aisle. It hit the floor and rolled on, stopping finally at Miss Brown's feet.

She did not smile at me now. The silence in the classroom was ominous, the awesome stillness of the air before the first clap of thunder. It was broken by one sharp command, "Pickitup!" The accompanying hand movement made the meaning clear. I raised myself very gradually. The clunk of the seat was deafening. It was the longest walk of my life. Step by step, I approached the incriminating inkwell at Miss Brown's pointing toe. My brown oxfords, which had seemed so elegant when we bought them in Vienna, betrayed me at every step, making hollow sounds like the white canes of those who can't see.

～

My neighbour Rita and I became friends the summer we were thirteen years old. She was taller than me and very blond, with Nordic blue eyes with a Slavic slant and wore a nylon bra under blouses and sweaters that clung. I had not yet acquired this American armature, a shield from and attraction for boys who loved to ping the elastic band in the back with wicked, knowing grins.

Rita knew all about boys. She even knew French-Canadian boys, different from the English-speaking boys I had met in Grade 7 at Iona Avenue School. Rita said the boy she was fixing me up with was not really French. That didn't make me feel less nervous about going to the baseball game on a double date. I knew nothing about baseball and not much about a date with boys. My only experience with dating had been with George that summer in Hungary. I realized I had a lot to learn in Canada.

I wore my new sundress, pale blue with wide shoulder straps and a short bolero, a little cover-up that could be hooked under a Peter Pan collar. I had chosen the pattern from a McCall fashion book at Marshall's on St. Catherine Street, where we went to buy materials and patterns for my mother to sew on her new electric Singer sewing machine. I had stood in front of the full-length mirror attached to the door of her bedroom while my mother pinned up the hem to make it even. I felt like one of the princesses I had drawn in class. We both admired my image as I twirled slowly on command.

After Rita rang my doorbell, I was less sure of the effect. Rita wore slacks and a tight white sweater. "Sexy" was one of the expressions I had learned. The disappointed look on my blind date's face was obvious and reinforced my doubts about the outfit. Serge and Rita sat close together on the hard, wooden bench of the jerking streetcar. He had his arm around her shoulders. My date and I sat far apart in silence. At the baseball game, Serge and Rita's intimate games absorbed them more than the one played on the dusty field below. I asked Serge's friend questions about the purpose of the strikes and runs and the meaning of foul ball, to which he mumbled inaudible replies with indifference. Things were not going well and only got worse when Serge made a snide joke in French to his bilingual friend, pointing to my well-developed, unshielded bosom. Following these remarks, I moved to sit at an even greater distance from my date and waited for the interminable innings to come to an end.

After this failed attempt at acculturation, Rita and I seldom met. Rita had eczema on her neck and on the inside of her elbow, and the cream she put on left a white powdery coating on her skin. She was "cheap" and "fast," my classmates in Grade 7 told me. I received a merit badge and a scholarship at the end of my first full school year and was promoted to the Latin class in high school. Rita was not promoted. Then we moved into a house, a duplex, and I went to a new school. We never saw each other again.

~

Ed was my first real boyfriend. I met him in Grade 8. He was older than the other boys my friends were dating because he was repeating the grade. It may have had something to do with his vision – one of his eyes seemed to wander in the opposite direction from the other. He was more like a man than a boy, compact and muscled. He kept his hands to himself in the movies and only held my hand in a respectful, clammy clutch in the dark or when we walked down the street.

We went to parties in my friends' musty, wood-panelled basements with Formica counter bars and danced close to "My Foolish Heart" and "Blue Moon," which were "my" songs. Ed didn't mind that I didn't know the steps of the foxtrot, couldn't keep the rhythm of the samba and kept his grip when he twirled me doing the jitterbug. He loved me all the same.

When I went to a private camp, Escobar, in the summer, he went to the YMCA camp Kanawana. He sent me long letters describing in detail his canoe trips in the wilderness of the Laurentian Mountains, illustrating the route with maps. He put three Xs for kisses under his name. I shared the letters with my bunkmates and called him a jerk, which made me feel important. By now I was in love with Roger, a counsellor who was the best baseball player at camp. I was only a counsellor-in-training, but I did have a day off. I shared the first one with Roger. We canoed across the lake to a private cove, where we swam and sunned ourselves on the beach. He kissed me, not quite as often or with as much intensity as I would have liked. We waited until the sun went down and cooked hot dogs and roasted marshmallows on the embers of the campfire Roger lit with expertise, then we paddled back to camp.

By that time my skin was livid red, a sunburn so painful that putting a shirt on my back was an excruciating experience. The Noxzema cream that was supposed to relieve my discomfort and prevent peeling only resulted in an unpleasant aura of camphor that trailed me wherever I went. Layers of my skin still hung in messy tatters for weeks. Roger went to the movies in Ste. Agathe with Risha on his next day off. She was pudgy but good-natured and played baseball well.

I cried a lot alone, muffling my sobs under the pillow at night. That night there was a social but I refused to go. I could hear the music from the recreation hall. They were playing "My Foolish Heart" – my song. I imagined Roger and Risha dancing close as Billy Eckstine crooned, "This time it isn't fascination." I took out Ed's last letter. And reread it. The words of the song fit my mood perfectly. "Or a dream that will fade and fall apart..." I reached for an unlined pad and my pen as the music ended after the line, "This time it's love, my foolish heart." I placed the ruled guide with blue lines under the first page and began to write,

Dear Ed,

Last week we canoed across the lake to a sandy beach. [I did not mention Roger.] *I was thinking of you as the paddle silently sliced the waves....*

I signed the letter with the word "love" and numerous Xs under my name.

Dead Man's Suit

Since coming to Canada, my father, who spoke ten languages and read avidly in at least four, had never found work appropriate to his intellectual interests. Unlike his two elder brothers in Hungary, he was not a successful businessman and had managed to fail at every commercial enterprise he undertook in Montreal. My father's last, in a series of unsuitable occupations, had been in a local hardware chain. As a salesman in the electrical department, he would explain with scholarly passion the functioning of any gadget in English or French, unaware of whether the customer seemed interested or was impatient to pay and leave the store. Nothing deterred my little father in his grey smock from exploring the essence of every problem, however trivial.

The first of his failed efforts had been the purchase of a small apartment building in which the tenants regularly neglected to pay their rent. Another venture was a fleet of taxis with whose drivers my father could easily banter in his recently acquired *joual*, the Québécois dialect. This did not deter the chauffeurs from fixing the metres so that eventually my father had to sell the cars at a considerable loss. Finally, he tried to establish a gourmet deli in the 1950s, when the shelves of supermarkets still satisfied Montrealers' needs for specialty foods.

Walking in the street, my father usually carried a European

briefcase with one of its two buckles carelessly undone. This way, passersby had an excellent view of the strange collection inside: a Chinese grammar, the daily paper intricately folded for reading on public transportation and a library book carefully covered in brown wrapping paper. My father had a profound respect for books. He also carried a writing pad for jotting down observations, and sometimes a package of sticky buns bought on sale at a local bakery. He'd forge ahead with small, energetic, bouncy steps, hitching up his left shoulder from time to time. In my teens, I did not appreciate his efforts to civilize me. I was into movie magazines and Mickey Spillane.

My father had never been easy to fit with ready-made clothes. In Hungary a tailor had catered to his special measurements. Now in Montreal he still had a few ancient European suits for formal wear, a three-quarter-length green loden coat acquired in Vienna on his way to the New World from Budapest, and a collection of bargain-store jackets for everyday. At my mother's urging, my father finally agreed to visit a tailor recommended by a friend. When they arrived at his workshop, the tailor seemed upset. One of his best customers had just died. This was sad news, especially since the new suit the man had recently ordered remained unpaid.

"Sir," the tailor said cheerfully, "the suit might just fit you! Try it on!"

It did. The double-breasted suit with the wide lapels fit as though it had been made to measure for my father. After this, whenever they needed to get dressed up, my mother would always remind him to wear *a halott öltönyét*. The dead man's suit. It became a family in-joke.

~

The year my father died in Montreal, in 1969, I was a graduate student at an American university in Michigan. I had married in 1957 and my husband, Tevia, and I had decided to return to graduate school in 1968, taking our two small sons, Ira and Eugene, with us to the Midwest. Just days before we were to leave Montreal, I had a distressing call from my mother.

"I have to tell you some bad news," she began, as though I were still a child to be sheltered from family problems. "Your father has cancer."

She said it in Hungarian: *Rák*. The same word for both the disease and the crustacean. It conjured up ill-omened images of crabs, tentacled, blindly crawling in the confines of a transparent water tank. At this time, in the 1960s, the diagnosis was usually fatal.

"How long does he have?" I asked her.

"Maybe six months, maybe less."

My father was not told this prognosis. At the time, it was thought best to spare the sick from knowing the worst truths about their condition. He was given some medication, released from the hospital and seemed to resume his normal life, except that he never went back to work, much to his relief.

When, on his doctor's recommendation, he quit Pascal's Hardware, he was able at last to devote all his time to the books, music and conversations he loved. These more often than not turned into monologues as he knew so much and had so much to say. Curiously, he had never quite acquired the listening skills necessary for casual communication.

We left Montreal while my father was in remission and in high spirits, studying the map of Michigan for landmarks to visit. On the dining-room table lay scattered maps and travel books he had borrowed from the library. Sitting in his armchair, he even seemed at that time to be a towering presence. When we returned from Michigan during the Thanksgiving break, however, I found that my father had been hospitalized again. A plastic bag suspended above his bed released its crystal globules to replace the food he used to enjoy with embarrassing gusto. In the elevated bed, he lay passive, not resisting with his body, only with his mind.

He couldn't talk because of the obstructing tubes, but in spite of that, his mind was vibrantly alive and he wrote furiously on the ruled spiral pad kept on the night table by his bed. In a strange script of crooked capital letters he wrote down historical facts he remembered, some familiar jokes and just one complaint, "MY FEET ARE COLD." A burly male nurse bent over his thin legs, a waxy yellow as they protruded from the covers.

"You must be chilly. I'll rub them for you," he offered.

The hospital room was overheated, but the numbing tentacles of the cancer had by then spread to every part of my father's body. The soothing movements of the practiced hands seemed to help him drift off to sleep. I looked more carefully at the other notes on the writing pad and recognized the fragment of a poem by Heinrich Heine, the nineteenth-century German poet, Jewish convert to Catholicism, whose iconoclastic spirit my father admired. I remembered the weekend mornings when, wearing the brown striped bathrobe my mother had made for him, my father would recite German poetry from one of the gilt-edged volumes lining his bookshelf. I had heard these lines so often that I did not need a translation.

Keine Messe wird man singen,
Keinen Kadosch wird man sagen,
Nichts gesagt, und nichts gesungen
Wird an meinen Sterbetagen.

No mass will be sung,
no prayers will be said,
nothing sung and nothing said
on the day of my death.

Making sure the notepad was within reach of his hand, next to the glasses my mother had carefully removed, I left. Only the light rise and fall of the white hospital gown indicated that he was still alive. He seemed so tiny in the tall, wide bed, almost like a little boy.

Michigan winters were cold, but over the phone came a chiller wind from Montreal the morning my mother called.

"I have very bad news."

"How long?" I asked, just as I had six months before.

"The doctors can't say. He's barely conscious now."

"I have a presentation tomorrow morning. What if I left at noon?" I needed to prolong the temporary, deceptive serenity of my academic routine.

"Do as you like!" The line went dead.

Landing at Dorval airport seemed to take forever. For one hopeful moment I looked to find a familiar face and, disappointed, went to the telephone. I dialed the hospital number. I asked for my father's room, visualizing the light rise and fall of the white hospital gown, the ever-present notepad and pen, a male nurse rubbing the poor, chilled feet, my mother sitting by the phone....

"Hello? It's me... I'm in Montreal."

There was silence at the other end, then a quick intake of breath, my mother's voice, "There's no need to rush anymore."

My father's funeral under a grey, cold February sky was a simple one: a few words, a few mumbled prayers as the coffin was slowly lowered into the icy ground. I stared at the plain pine coffin, imagining my father in it, wearing the "dead man's suit." Clean-shaven, dapper and silent as he never was in life.

My Mother's Secrets

I began to appreciate my mother twenty years after her death, on a guided tour of Lithuania, a country she had never seen. My mother's last days in 1984 had been spent at a small, genteel hospital in Montreal, in a room with just one window, shaded by the lush, late summer leaves of the tree growing outside. I visited her, staying for long, quiet hours, offering soup and sips of water. I tried, but failed, to feel genuine grief in my heart as I sat in the visitor's armchair facing her bed.

She seemed so diminutive in the hospital bed. Cancer had wasted her body, leaving unaltered in the small, bony frame only the spirit that still glowed in her morphine-bright eyes. Her face had become pale and waxy, no longer matted by the rosy layer of the powder she used to apply daily with a fuzzy pink puff, the powder whose musty aroma I had inhaled with secret pleasure as a small child. Her only other concession to cosmetics had been a conventional orange-red shade of lipstick. Without it, her lips were fever-chapped and white. Her hair, a natural dark brown, never dyed, remained the same as ever, full and glossy, with hardly any white showing at seventy-four. By styling it herself, she had saved money, time and the need to submit to a stranger's touch. My mother had always flinched from physical contact, even mine. The cheek she turned to me for a formal kiss on greeting or parting always seemed impassive and cool.

She had always been a small woman. In my teens I was already almost eight centimetres taller than her and weighed considerably more; especially during the time I used food as my consolation for pain and loneliness. I was larger only physically. My mother's short, wiry body was a giant and indomitable tower of strength. With our growing inequality in size, our less tangible differences also grew. We were increasingly disappointed in each other.

I know she did love me when I was small. "Before you were born, I knew you'd be a girl, a Judit," she'd say. She copied my first words in a scrapbook that survived the war in Hungary and accompanied us to Canada. She also kept the poems she had written to me during the year we were separated, she in Bergen-Belsen and I first in the convent and later in Mária's apartment. She often told me about the cold night in Bergen-Belsen when she gave up her blanket to a little girl whose name was Judit like mine, offering it in the hope that others would give me, who was then so far from her, a warm cover when I needed one. Her sacrifice seemed to work; thanks to the nuns and our friend Mária, I did survive. I often wondered whether I'd have been ready to do what she had.

My mother didn't speak about her experiences during the deportation except to recall episodes when she had proven herself generous and brave, like giving up her blanket on that particular freezing night. She told of times she had successfully deceived the SS officer in charge of the daily roll call by helping to hide my cousin Imi, a boy of thirteen, so he would not be taken away from his mother and sister to the men's barracks. She told the story of that kerchiefed boy among the women with self-deprecating humour. Just another battle she had won. She was the shining star in whose reflected glory I should have been happy to bask, but was not.

Then, after she died, as I was clearing out her room, I found carefully wrapped in tissue paper at the bottom of a drawer a heart-shaped silk picture frame awkwardly stitched by me, my photograph in the middle. The note with it was addressed to "Anyucim" (my little mother) and ended with "Sok-sok puszi" (many, many kisses). Dated May 1948, it was the Mother's Day gift I had given her when I was in Grade 5. We left Hungary that fall.

When did my feelings change?

As my father's business ventures failed one by one, the funds we had managed to bring with us from Hungary trickled away. Just as she had tried to protect me from the consequences of my Jewish identity when I was seven, my mother attempted to keep from me the reality of our economic free fall, that we had become impoverished foreigners. My mother's struggles against bills and disappearing savings were stories she didn't feel proud of, or was too proud to tell.

My father was humbled by the changes. When they married, my parents were the same height. As he sank into depression, my father seemed to shrink and age. While he took refuge in books, I indulged in the soporific pleasure of chocolate-coated marshmallow cookies and potato chips to mitigate my resentment and shame. Only my mother remained undeterred. I hated the sequined satin collars she sewed and tried to sell, the blue cotton uniform she wore during my father's last investment, a deli on Monkland Avenue around the corner from our house where my classmates' parents, to my embarrassment, sometimes went to buy a quart of milk or a loaf of bread.

When that enterprise, too, went bankrupt, my mother took a job filing papers in the office of Steinberg's, a Canadian grocery chain. Her unusual English notwithstanding (my mother didn't have my father's or my knack for languages) she managed to earn a diploma at night school and advanced from filing clerk to become the firm's librarian. There were no blankets large enough to wrap around the cold child who had turned into an oversized adolescent; no time to write poems to her. She still loved me, she said, and added with a smile, in French with the Hungarian accent I found so embarrassing, "Ce n'est pas le Pérou, mais c'est à moi." (No treasure, but she's mine.) Her disappointment in me was evident in every impatient look and gesture. My relationship with her had hardened into an impenetrable wall of passive resistance.

For many years, I ignored my father's lectures on literature and the heroes of European history. I ridiculed the postcard collection of famous works of art he had backed with shirt cardboards for display. On entering college, books, history and art began to engage me too and we finally had common themes to talk to each other about.

With the passing of the years, I had mellowed. I had found many friends, a profession, and as teacher, wife and mother I was determined not to dwell on the past that had set me apart from the inhabitants of a warless world. I didn't visit the Holocaust museums in Washington or New York, avoided reading the wrenching biographies of victims of the Holocaust, World War II and its aftermath. I chose to ignore the terrible reality my mother's anecdotes masked for my benefit, and perhaps also for her own.

Then, a few years ago, my husband and I joined friends to tour the Baltic countries, a part of Europe I had never visited before. It was in Vilnius, the capital of Lithuania, that I began to enter my mother's past.

On our first afternoon we stopped in an old prison, now called the Museum of Genocide Victims. It had been the headquarters of the Communist secret police during two Soviet occupations, where anyone suspected of activities hostile to the regime was tortured, sentenced and, if found guilty, executed immediately in an underground chamber. The thick padding on that door was to muffle the shots and screams. Taking the grisly tour, I remembered the spring day in 1948 when the two men in belted raincoats had come to the door of our apartment in Budapest to take my mother in for questioning.

The Holocaust Museum was next on our agenda. In the entrance hall of the museum, we saw a family portrait, three generations of Lithuanian Jews, twenty or so smiling people, posed for the unseen photographer. Circles had been drawn around two of the faces, the only two who had survived the war said the key. I entered the last room with trepidation, like Judith in Bluebeard's castle facing the door she must not unlock, knowing that she would. There it was, the photograph of the naked women on their way to the pits in the forest near Vilnius, urged on by armed men in uniform. A row of soldiers, with guns pointed, stood facing the pit, ready to shoot. In the background lounged more soldiers, their guns idle, casually smoking, chatting, relaxed. The women didn't look like the skeletal scarecrows in pictures of the last inhabitants of concentration camps. They were full-breasted – mothers and grandmothers. Their thighs were still fleshy, almost alive.

I thought of the naked women in twos and threes, lining up to shower in Bergen-Belsen, imagining my mother, a thin, naked shape, my mother who would only undress behind a beach towel, unseen, in the changing room of a public pool. On the way to the bathhouse in the camp, my mother recalled, it was never clear whether the showerheads would release water or poison gas. The point of her story was not the degradation or the fear, but that she, her sister, her niece and even the nephew she had helped to camouflage by tying a kerchief on his head, all survived. Such a victory!

On my next trip to Montreal I made one of my infrequent visits to the Jewish cemetery in the Town of Mount Royal. I picked up two smooth, worn pebbles and placed one on my father's and the other on my mother's grave. The tombstones were identical grey granite but, I hadn't realized this before, only my father had a footstone, engraved with his name, date of birth and death, their memories as unequal in the afterlife as they had been in my affections.

I searched for words with which to acknowledge my mother, the way I had come to know her, not in Hungary or Canada, but in Lithuania, where she had never been. The ones I finally chose to have chiselled on the stone came from a short story I remembered reading in high school. In it a prisoner waiting for execution quotes from Shakespeare's *Julius Caesar*: "The valiant never taste of death but once."

One of the Lucky Ones

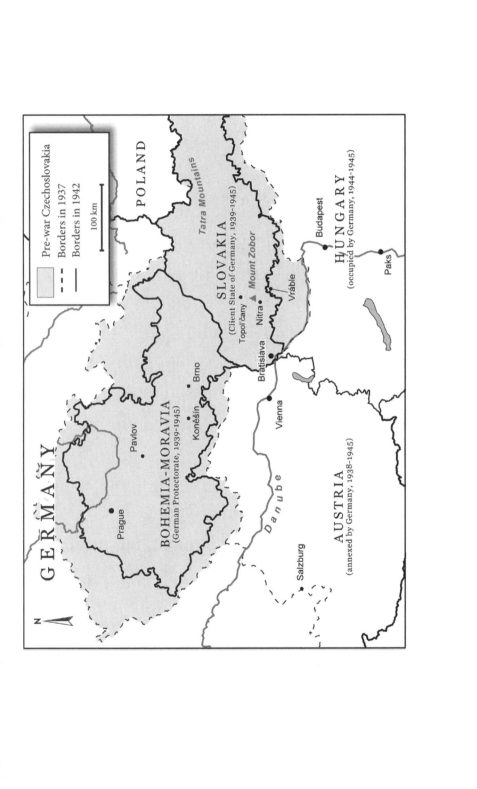

GERMANY

POLAND

BOHEMIA-MORAVIA
(German Protectorate, 1939–1945)

Prague

Pavlov

Koněšín

Brno

Tatra Mountains

SLOVAKIA
(Client State of Germany, 1939–1945)

Topoľčany

Nitra

Mount Zobor

Vráble

Bratislava

Vienna

AUSTRIA
(annexed by Germany, 1938–1945)

Salzburg

Danube

HUNGARY
(occupied by Germany, 1944–1945)

Budapest

Paks

N

Pre-war Czechoslovakia
Borders in 1937
Borders in 1942

100 km

Eva Marx's Family Tree*

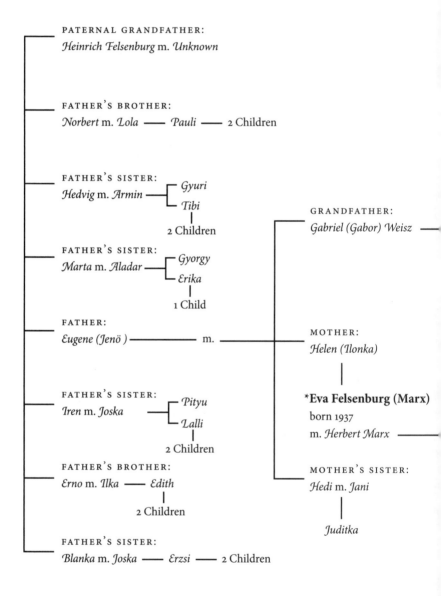

PATERNAL GRANDFATHER:
Heinrich Felsenburg m. *Unknown*

FATHER'S BROTHER:
Norbert m. *Lola* —— *Pauli* —— 2 Children

FATHER'S SISTER:
Hedvig m. *Armin* ⎡ *Gyuri*
⎣ *Tibi*
|
2 Children

GRANDFATHER:
Gabriel (Gabor) Weisz ——

FATHER'S SISTER:
Marta m. *Aladar* ⎡ *Gyorgy*
⎣ *Erika*
|
1 Child

FATHER:
Eugene (Jenö) —————— m. ——

MOTHER:
Helen (Ilonka)

*Eva Felsenburg (Marx)
born 1937
m. *Herbert Marx* ——

FATHER'S SISTER:
Iren m. *Joska* ⎡ *Pityu*
⎣ *Lalli*
|
2 Children

MOTHER'S SISTER:
Hedi m. *Jani*
|
Juditka

FATHER'S BROTHER:
Erno m. *Ilka* —— *Edith*
|
2 Children

FATHER'S SISTER:
Blanka m. *Joska* —— *Erzsi* —— 2 Children

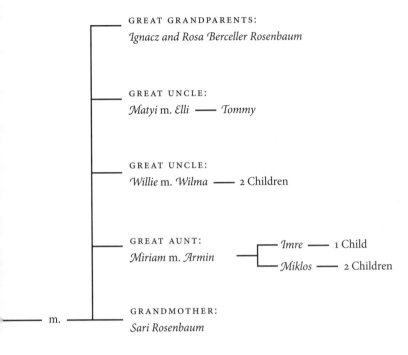

GREAT GRANDPARENTS:
Ignacz and Rosa Berceller Rosenbaum

GREAT UNCLE:
Matyi m. *Elli* —— *Tommy*

GREAT UNCLE:
Willie m. *Wilma* —— 2 Children

GREAT AUNT:
Miriam m. *Armin*
— *Imre* —— 1 Child
— *Miklos* —— 2 Children

m. —

GRANDMOTHER:
Sari Rosenbaum

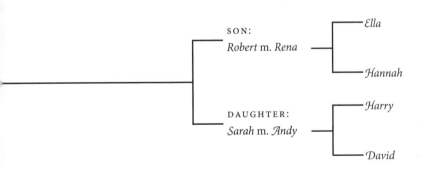

SON:
Robert m. *Rena*
— *Ella*
— *Hannah*

DAUGHTER:
Sarah m. *Andy*
— *Harry*
— *David*

I would like to express my deep appreciation to my husband, Herbert Marx, who encouraged and helped me in writing this memoir. It is dedicated with love to our children Robert, Rena, Sarah and Andy and to our grandchildren Ella, Hannah, Harry and David.

Brno

I was one of the lucky ones. Jewish children living in Europe were undoubtedly the most vulnerable victims in Hitler's design to annihilate the Jewish people. Almost 1.6 million children were living in Europe at the start of World War II. By the end of the war, less than 500,000 had survived. Most of these children had been left orphans, scarred by the trauma of the Holocaust, and bereft of family or friends to guide them as they confronted uncertain futures. Although I lost my grandparents and many other relatives, I was saved, and my parents were saved along with me.

I was born in Brno, in the Moravian region of Czechoslovakia on October 21, 1937, the only child of Eugene (Jenö) Felsenburg and Helen (Ilonka) Weisz. My parents moved to Brno from Slovakia because Brno was regarded as an enlightened place of opportunity. At the time, Slovakia was not industrialized or as developed as Moravia, its neighbour to the west; most of Slovakia's economy was based on agriculture. Both my parents were born in small, rural Slovak townships – my mother came from Vráble, my father from Topoľčany – that nevertheless had sizeable Jewish communities, with synagogues and Hebrew schools.

Brno (or Brunn in German) was the capital of Moravia, now part of the Czech Republic. Moravia, the central region of what was then Czechoslovakia, is flanked by Bohemia to the west and the White

Carpathian Mountains to the east. The mountains provide a natural border between Moravia and Slovakia; on the northern side, the Sudetes Mountains, from which the "Sudeten Deutsch" (ethnic German) residents of Moravia get their name, form the border between Moravia and Poland. Situated approximately 120 kilometres from Vienna, the Austrian-German influence in Brno was strongly felt. From the seventeenth century, as part of the Austro-Hungarian Empire under the Hapsburg rule, nearly the entire upper and middle classes of Brno were either German or German-speaking. Many Sudeten-Deutsch Germans lived and worked in Brno and had a natural allegiance to Germany. This German element played a critical role in Czechoslovakia during the war. When Hitler came to power, his policies received an immediate and enthusiastic reception in Brno, even before Germany annexed most of Czechoslovakia in 1938.

As far back as 1229, however, Brno's ancient charter was a model of liberal town government. In 1243, King Wenceslas made it a free city with an open outlook to the world. Brno also served as Napoleon's headquarters during the battle of Austerlitz in 1805. The city was highly industrialized and even today holds a large annual international trade fair. We were proud of Brno's landmarks, fine examples of gothic and baroque architecture. A music conservatory and several fine museums, theatre and opera houses are located in the city. The Spielberg Castle, situated on the Brno Mountain, graces the centre of the city, much like Montreal's Mount Royal, where I now live. The castle has a notorious past: its dungeon, now a tourist site, housed the Hapsburg's most terrifying prison. Brno was also the location of notable educational institutions, such as Masaryk University, where my cousins Peter and Pista Seltzer came to study medicine, and the famous Beneš Technical College. In fact, the father of modern genetics, Gregor Mendel, did his seminal work in Brno in the 1800s. Sadly, the city's impressive cultural heritage could not shield it from being swept up in World War II.

When he married my mother, my father had already apprenticed with his uncle Morris Felsenburg, who had a prosperous fur enterprise in Berlin. While he was there, he not only learned the trade, but also perfected his German-language skills, of which he was very proud. German was very fashionable and important to know, speak and understand throughout the Czech lands. Hungarian was the dominant language of influence in Slovakia, which, under the Austro-Hungarian Empire, had been part of Hungary. My mother also spoke and read German tolerably well, but the mother tongue of both my parents was Hungarian. They both initially went to Hungarian schools, switching to Slovak instruction when the map of Europe was re-drawn after World War I.

Before the war, my parents struggled to establish themselves in business in Brno. With hard work and help from my mother, my father opened two fur stores: one across from the railroad station in Brno and another concession or boutique at Dom Moderné Brněnký (DMB) – "The House of the Modern Brnoesse." The DMB, situated in a stately building on Masarykova Street in the heart of Brno, was the only large department store in the city at the time. As in Paris and other European cities, an apartment dwelling on a busy, elegant street was very desirable and it was convenient and practical for my parents to move onto the fourth floor of the same building that the DMB occupied. We used a separate entrance and elevator that was completely independent from the store.

There were three apartments on our floor. The superintendents of the building, Mr. and Mrs. Bumbalek, lived right next to us and down the hall lived Gerti and Frantisek Kadlec, who were good friends of ours. I am still in contact with their son, Jiři. The Kadlecs' union was a mixed marriage and Mrs. Kadlec's elderly Jewish parents lived with them. The Jewish part of the family was totally assimilated; they ate pork and kept no particular Jewish customs. This was not uncommon among Czech Jews, many of whom had strong national allegiances and tried to blend in with the Czech-German populations and their culture. I recall many friendly visits with the Kadlec family, who lived so close to us. They had a large corner apartment and a baby grand piano, which Mrs. Kadlec played well while her father accompanied her on his violin.

Our apartment, though not as large and elegant as the Kadlecs', was spacious, with large rooms connected by French doors. After the war, when my parents reclaimed it, a swing was installed for me in the entryway between the living room and the large room next to it. We had two balconies, one in the front and one off the kitchen in the back. There was a maid's room ("Everyone had a maid," my mother always said) and I had my own small room. It was a comfortable home. I remember feeling cozy and safe in my bed as I listened to the noise of the streetcars and the hum of the traffic below.

My parents' was an arranged marriage. They were introduced by my mother's uncle Matyi, who was friendly with my father. Even after they were married, there was not much time for romance. My mother was a working woman, helping my father in the two stores. As was often the custom then, my mother brought a maid from Vráble, a very devoted, hard-working and trustworthy person named Marka Piesikova. She helped with the housework and, when I came along, she took care of me while my mother was at work.

My father realized how lucky he was in his choice of a mate. Not only was my mother beautiful, intelligent and industrious, she had also studied fine embroidery and haute couture in Budapest as a young girl. She was an expert seamstress, which was to come in handy in the fur trade later on. She, too, had lived with relatives during the three years of her apprenticeship in Budapest, where she studied and learned the fine art of sewing and needlework.

My mother told me that some of her happiest memories were of those years in Budapest. She boarded with her aunt Miriam (Miriam néni in Hungarian) and two mischievous cousins, Miklos and Imre, who were my mother's age. The three young people enjoyed theatre, music and all the abundant culture that the very sophisticated Budapest had to offer at the time. But above all, she loved her cousins' company. They were very proud of her beauty and she often said that she never laughed so much as when she was with them; they loved playing tricks and harmless pranks and telling uproarious jokes.

As it was in those days, when my mother reached the age of twenty-two her family thought it was "high time to get married." Although my mother had been in love with Dr. Rafman, Vráble's eligible, young Jewish doctor, "He didn't marry me," she said. "And anyway," she rationalized, "he wasn't religious enough for my father." He married his gentile nurse, but their union didn't save him. He perished in the Holocaust.

My maternal grandfather, an honourable and respected grain merchant in Vráble who had married happily through an arranged marriage himself, "put his foot down," as my mother often said. In those days, there weren't many choices for a respectable, young Jewish woman outside of matrimony. My grandfather, therefore, pressured my mother into marriage.

My father was distinguished in appearance and came from a good family. My mother often retold the story of how my dad deliberately missed his train back to Budapest, where he lived and worked at the time, when he came to Vráble to "look her over" – as was the custom with arranged marriages. He wanted to spend more time with her. After a brief courtship, my parents were married.

My parents' marriage was not a union made in heaven. Not only were they complete opposites in temperament, their backgrounds were very different as well. My father was tall and blue-eyed (often mistaken for a German during and after the war), while my mother was a delicate beauty with soft brown eyes, a *schön Judin*, a "Jewish beauty" as her gentile doctor in Brno called her. My father was always on the move, an extrovert with an unpredictable temper that was easily ignited. She was calm, introverted and a reader. She loved books and especially enjoyed the English writers such as Dickens – she read all his books. Rudyard Kipling's *Jungle Book* was her favourite. She told me that she had even read all of Shakespeare's plays. "Reading was my salvation," she often said.

My mother came from a very close, harmonious family. She was the eldest of two sisters and adored her younger sister, Hedi. "She was the smarter one, but I was the beauty!" she would say. My mother, though, was a very good student. "I did my work and what I was told," she told me. She dreamed of becoming a teacher. When she could not pursue this career for herself her ambitions fell on me, her child.

My father's family, on the other hand, was a raucous one. Tragically, they had lost their mother when my father was very young and his six siblings always fought and argued amongst themselves. There had been three other children who had died in infancy. My paternal grandfather never remarried. He was a harsh and strict disciplinarian, which resulted in my father and grandfather not speaking to each other. Financial burdens added to the stressful family life. My grandfather's business venture – a margarine factory in Topoľčany – had failed, plunging the family into bankruptcy.

At the young age of eighteen, my father was conscripted into the Austro-Hungarian army during World War I, and when the war was over, he more or less walked all the way home from Italy. It was his misfortune to suffer through two world wars and a most difficult, insecure life; these things, no doubt, affected his frayed and nervous temperament.

So it was that circumstances united two such different natures from very different backgrounds. My parents' married life was filled with tensions and economic constraints made their existence extremely difficult even before war broke out. Both partners worked very hard to establish a business and to make a living. After the German annexation of the Sudetenland in September 1938 and the invasion of Czechoslovakia in 1939, however, life became impossible.[1]

---

1   For information on annexation of the Sudetenland, as well as other significant historical events; major organizations and people; geographical locations; religious and cultural terms; and foreign-language words and expressions contained in the text, please see the glossary.

Caught up in the euphoria of Hitler's goal of a united Germany under the motto "Deutschland über alles" (Germany above all), the German population of Brno adopted the attitudes of their fatherland and became virulently antisemitic.

My father was attuned to what was happening around him. Although he had always praised the German customers who came to him as most pleasant and cooperative, he noticed a drastic change in their behaviour and saw the handwriting on the wall. He realized that he and his small family would have to leave Brno as soon as possible. My mother always credited my father for his keen instinct of self-preservation. "He saved our lives," she said. "Without him we wouldn't be here."

My First Escape

Following the German invasion of Czechoslovakia in March 1939, the Nazis divided the country. They established the Protectorate of Bohemia and Moravia – which included Brno – under direct occupation, while Slovakia became a semi-autonomous protectorate governed by the openly pro-Nazi Hlinka's Slovak People's Party (HSSP) and its president, Father Jozef Tiso. Almost immediately, the military arm of the HSSP, Slovakia's notorious and antisemitic Hlinka Guard, made conditions difficult for Jewish citizens. They began harassing Jews and desecrating cemeteries and synagogues, and the Slovakian government began passing anti-Jewish laws in April 1939, only one month into their mandate. In September 1939, Slovakia entered the war as an ally of Hitler's Third Reich.

Concerned about what was happening, my father's first act was to dispatch me with our faithful and loving maid, Marka, to my maternal grandparents, Sari and Gabriel Weisz, in Vráble, Slovakia. The southern part of Slovakia, where Vráble was located, had been annexed by Hungary just prior to the German occupation and breakup of Czechoslovakia. As a result, it was much safer there. At the time of the journey, I was two years old. Marka had never married and perhaps regarded me as the child she never had. I can still feel the unconditional and genuine affection and love that she gave me. I boarded a train with Marka from Brno to Vráble and have a vague memory of that journey. If the Germans, who interrogated everyone, asked about our identities, I was to say that Marka was my mother. Our story was that we were returning home after visiting her family in Brno. I still remember the small brown fur coat and matching hat with little ears that I wore on the train.

Next, my father asked a couple of business associates he hoped he could trust to run his two businesses for him in Brno. My parents then left Brno and became drifters without a home or fixed destination. For the duration of the war they moved from one place to another. After September 9, 1941, Czechoslovakian Jews were forced to sew a Star of David onto their outside clothing so that they were easily identifiable in public. My father took off their stars on their many travels.

Living as non-Jews required false identity papers, which were difficult to obtain in German-occupied Europe. Identification papers were also subject to constant scrutiny by the authorities. Jews could sometimes obtain legitimate documents under an assumed name. Both these ruses posed great risks to the bearer since Germans and collaborating police forces monitored the population so closely.

As far as I know, my parents had no false papers. They did, however, keep on the move, travelling from place to place. More than once, they bribed a conductor to let them get off a train when they saw German soldiers asking people for their identification papers. My parents became nomads. To avoid detection, they split up and travelled separately, staying wherever they could – with relatives, acquaintances, and once even at a rabbi's home – avoiding the Germans and making their way as far as Budapest. At the same time, my father was constantly on the lookout, trying to arrange a permanent hiding place for all of us.

During that period of about five years, from 1939 to 1944, I stayed with my mother's parents in Vráble while Marka lived with her family at the other end of town. This separation tormented my parents and me, but there was nothing else they could do.

I have many memories of my life in Vráble. I remember my maternal grandparents as rather distant. My grandfather was bald and slim with a neatly trimmed moustache. He was a grain merchant, and was often away on business trips to Bratislava, Slovakia's capital, or to Nitra, a neighbouring Slovak city that was to play a key role in the survival of my family. I can't really remember much communication with him. He was introverted by nature and was not well. He had suffered an injury in World War I and apparently never regained his strength. My grandmother always cooked special food for him, keeping him on a strict diet prescribed for his condition.

Quite miraculously, my grandfather's life was saved during World War I by a prayer book he always carried in his pocket. He was shot while serving as a soldier in the Austro-Hungarian army under the Emperor Franz Jozef, but the bullet, instead of going into my grandfather's flesh, lodged in the book. We still have this prayer book, bullet hole and all, as a treasured family heirloom. Contributing to my grandfather's ill health was the fact that he maintained a strictly kosher diet, following the Jewish dietary laws. In order to ensure that he didn't accidentally eat non-kosher meat during the war, he refrained from eating meat of any kind; it depleted his physical strength but not his moral fortitude or mental discipline.

In contrast, my grandmother was more outgoing and less religious, although she strictly observed all the Jewish Orthodox traditions. While my grandfather was fighting at the front during World War I, to make ends meet she managed a candy store. Short and stout, with white hair pulled into a bun, she was strict and had little time for me. She was a strong-willed woman who ran a busy household with a "staff" of peasant girls and women. She had false teeth, which I found fascinating because they made a clicking sound that I liked and tried to imitate. I remember that every morning I had to sit on a potty and "produce." This took a long time and I recall circling around the large kitchen dragging along the large round pan that I sat on.

I also remember visiting Marka and her large, extended kin.

Whenever they cured pork after butchering a large sow, they had a celebration and I was invited to the feast. I loved the ham and sausages that were served. I could indulge without any guilt as my grandmother turned a blind eye and let me enjoy these non-kosher treats. In my life outside the perimeter of her household, I enjoyed total freedom.

I loved swinging on the tall swing suspended from a sturdy branch near Marka's house and, best of all, going swimming in the small Žitava River and picnicking with Marka and her nieces and nephews. They used to bring melons and submerge them in Žitava's waters to keep them cool and fresh. I relished the splashing and the summer fun with Marka watching nearby.

Marka was deeply religious. Every Sunday she attended Catholic mass and brought me along with her nieces and nephews. I remember admiring the beautiful gothic church full of colour, statues and religious artifacts. I was accepted as one of the worshippers, although everyone must have known that I was Jewish. My mother used to say that the kind priest's housekeeper, whose name was Livora Herman, was his girlfriend! How strange that this kind of gossip is still retained by fickle memory.

My grandmother was what we call in Yiddish an excellent *balebusteh* (homemaker) and *beryeh* (well-organized and efficient). I recall her directing the many different people who worked for her. Her pretty house was immaculate. There was a piano in the living room (my mother and her sister both had piano lessons) and the shelves held many books, both secular and Hebrew prayer books. We ate in the sunny dining room. Lunch was the main meal of the day and on the Sabbath, delicious *cholent*, which was a meat and bean stew, was brought from the baker's oven where it had simmered overnight. It was golden in colour with a mouth-watering aroma that I loved. I also looked forward to my grandmother's carp, a fish that she bought live and placed in a tub of water. Under my grandmother's supervision, it was cleaned and prepared to perfection, served cold in its own jelly, sweetened and sprinkled with nuts.

I slept in a small room at the back of the house and, in spite of the house being relatively modern, there was no indoor plumbing. Instead, there was a wooden outhouse connected to the rest of the building by a balcony so that we didn't actually have to step outside the premises.

My grandmother tended an extensive garden with her staff. There was a lovely flower garden in the front of the house, where a benign guard dog named Morza Kutya (Crumb Dog) had his doghouse. Of course, he was never allowed indoors as his role was strictly defined: to guard the house behind the large wrought-iron gates. There was also an extensive vegetable garden as well as a fruit garden with strawberries, gooseberries and apple and pear trees that reached all the way down to a little rivulet at the back of the property. I remember throwing pebbles in the water with my little friends and picking gooseberries. We would indulge ourselves on the tart green berries I loved.

Because the road in front of the house wasn't paved, every Saturday afternoon our peasant, farm-working neighbours would come out with long brooms made of thin branches tied together at one end. They would first sprinkle water on the dusty road and then sweep down the pathway. The kids loved to pitch in and we had lots of fun doing this clean-up together. Afterward, I was invited into their mud-floored cottages where they would offer me home-baked bread that had been lightly soaked in water and drizzled with sugar. It was a delicacy that I still remember. As far as I could tell I was accepted as an equal by the children and their parents.

I had many friends from the neighbouring peasant families in Vráble. We played freely in the fields and gardens and at the small brook that ran behind the house. I even remember playing "doctor" and once being knocked down by an iron handle that was used for pumping well-water. I ran under it when it was up and it came crashing down on my forehead. I still have a small scar to show for it. I also tried to swing from a clothesline strung up on my grandmother's balcony and landed face down on the gravel below with the small stones embedded painfully in my skin.

But my most embarrassing experience occurred when I was playing in the fields with my friends. We were running up and down haystacks, having a great time, when I ran up one of the small hay-covered mounds and sank into a smelly, soft heap. It was manure! Indistinguishable to me from the other haystacks, it was fertilizer of the natural kind, covered with hay – and I was immersed in it. How mortified I was and how ashamed! To add insult to injury, my strict grandmother was furious and scrubbed me from head to foot.

My mother occasionally visited me in Vráble and we would sometimes travel together to Budapest and Paks, a small Hungarian river town about 120 kilometres south of Budapest along the Danube. I remember the excitement of the voyage down the river on a large steamboat with my mother. I ran and played on the spacious deck of the boat and I had a wonderful time in Paks. It was the home of my maternal great-grandparents and many of my mother's Rosenbaum relatives. I do recall how I enjoyed being with all the aunts and uncles and getting lots of attention and love.

My mother's grandparents owned a printing press and printing business in Paks. They were so religious that on Saturdays the newspapers were put out for people to take but not sold because my great-grandparents would not handle money on the Sabbath. Instead, they trusted their customers to simply leave their money on a tray. I used to play on an iron circular stairway at their house. It wound, coil-like, from the family quarters on the first floor to their printing business on the second. I also remember falling from these stairs and bleeding badly. My great-grandfather's bed had the reputation of healing its occupant, so whenever one of the numerous children or grandchildren fell ill or was hurt, he or she went to sleep in great-grandfather's bed – this is where I, too, recovered.

My great-grandmother was an extremely devoted and fortunate parent. Not one of her nine children had died, a great distinction at a time when infant mortality was high. She never left the house, staying at home to tend to her large brood. Her daughters – my grandmother, Sari, and her younger sister, Miriam (Miriam néni), did not want this lifestyle. They both opted for small families, choosing to have only two children each. My mother used to tell me that Miriam néni's means of contraception was frequent abortions. Although outwardly observant, the two sisters were very practical and down to earth in their approach to religion.

Another memory I have from those visits was having fun in a large tin tub filled with water that sat in my great-grandparents' expansive cobblestone courtyard. Overall, those were happy times for me, surrounded by a jolly, extensive family that loved me. Recently, my mother's cousin, Joshua Ronn (né Rosenbaum), made a pilgrimage of sorts to his hometown of Paks, where he found not a trace of the flourishing Jewish community. Only a neglected and overgrown Jewish cemetery bears witness to its former existence.

On another occasion, we made a trip to Budapest that I remember vividly. I had fallen gravely ill with a high fever and developed whooping cough. I had to breathe deeply over a basin of hot water, my head under a towel so that I would get the benefit of the steam treatment. During this difficult time, in the midst of the war, all my mother's relatives pitched in to help us. My mother and I stayed in Budapest with her uncle, Willie Rosenbaum, and both my mother and father's families brought us food and even treats such as chocolate, a rare treasure in those days. In spite of my illness, I enjoyed being pampered. On these trips I travelled with my mother and was then returned to my grandparents in Vráble. I don't know the details of why we made these trips or the exact dates of the excursions; perhaps my parents were testing the waters to see where they could settle safely for the duration of the war.

～

One night after I had been in Vráble for about five years I had a nightmare. In my dream, buildings were burning, houses were on fire and smoke and flames were everywhere. I don't know whether it was a premonition of things to come, but I do remember it very clearly. Soon after that dream, in the spring of 1944, my grandmother bid me goodbye.

My grandparents had hired a man to take me by bicycle from Vráble to Nitra, twenty kilometres away, where I was to meet my father under a bridge. My grandmother had tears in her eyes as she prepared me for this unusual trip. I was alarmed that my stern, nonsense grandmother was so upset. She dressed me in peasant clothes with a kerchief tied under my chin, outfitting me in layers of full, colourful skirts, one on top of the other, in the Slovak country style. Then she embraced me and held me tight. I felt her tears dampen my cheek and felt inexplicably sad. I didn't really know why I was being sent away.

Thus disguised to avoid detection from German soldiers, I sat nervous and apprehensive on the rod of the man's bicycle the whole way, a trip that lasted perhaps two hours. My grandparents must have gotten word that the Jews in Vráble were going to be rounded up. Or, perhaps, just in the nick of time my father, by luck and pluck, had made arrangements for a hiding place for the three of us.

On June 10, 1944, soon after I left, the remaining 252 Jews of Vráble were sent to the ghetto in Levice, Slovakia; three days later, they were deported to Auschwitz. Tragically, my poor grandparents perished in the Holocaust, as did most of the Jews of Vráble, leaving not a trace of their small community.

~

I don't remember much about my reunion with my father under that bridge on the outskirts of Nitra. I was almost seven years old and hadn't seen my father in five years. I didn't even know what he looked like. I don't know all the details of my parents' lives prior to meeting up with my father that day. At that stage of my young life, he was a total stranger to me. He had probably chosen Nitra, a small city of 15,000, because he had some business connections there and a very close first cousin, Nandor Felsenburg, who was the town engineer. Nandor had come to Brno to study at the university and my father had helped him financially to complete his studies. Now, perhaps, my father hoped to get some assistance in return. My father also called on his associates in the fur trade in Nitra for help.

Nandor had procured a hiding place for himself, his wife, Herta, and small daughter, Eva, in a country farmhouse in the area near Mount Zobor, four kilometres outside Nitra. They hoped that this would prove safer than staying in the city. Alas, this was not to be the safe haven Nandor had hoped. One day the Germans came calling and took Nandor and his wife away. The farmer managed to hide their daughter by passing her off as his own child. Nandor survived Auschwitz, but Herta sadly perished. Eva, sheltered by the farmer and his wife, was reunited with her father after the war.

The time we spent waiting for my mother to join me and my father in Nitra was an uncomfortable period. At first I was boarded with a large woman I called Tamaci néni, where I felt especially ill at ease. I remember the insecure feeling I had living alone with her. My father was in hiding elsewhere. Then I was moved to another place, this time with a middle-aged Jewish woman. I remember one unfortunate incident when I spilled some hot oil from the stove onto the floor. The pot handle was protruding and I somehow bumped into it, spilling its contents. Although it was an accident, the woman treated the incident as a major calamity caused deliberately by me. I still remember her anger and threats as she cleaned up the mess. She told my father about what happened and I was made to feel guilty and ashamed.

I recall how nervous I was waiting for my mother's return every day that summer. I hadn't seen her in a very long time. What would I say to her? What would she be like? But what followed was liberation. Being reunited with my loving, understanding, gentle mother was like heaven. I never again felt lonely or abandoned, no matter how difficult or perilous the circumstances that followed. She was my guardian angel who supported me and protected me from all harm.

In Hiding

By the summer of 1944, finding a place for all three of us to hide was particularly challenging. Resistance against the German occupation in Slovakia was mounting and an uprising against the Slovak regime began in late August 1944. To suppress it, German troops moved in and ramped up their persecution of Slovakian Jews, rounding up thousands to be sent to concentration camps.

The stakes were high for individuals who sheltered Jews – those who were willing to take the chance put their own families in peril and faced the risk of arrest and severe punishment. Many Jewish families like ours continued to hope that they could wait out the war, anticipating that a time would soon come when they would no longer be targeted for death. Yet, even in those places where anti-Nazi sentiments were most vehement, the unfortunate reality was that the willingness to save Jews in Slovakia was never as ardent as the willingness to see them gone. There were unfortunate stories of people who swindled Jews out of their savings, promising to help them for a fee before reporting them to the Gestapo, the Nazi secret police. Many others started off with good intentions but ended up turning out Jews they had previously helped out of anxiety or fear.

My mother had grave doubts about the hiding place my father found. It was located on the main street of Nitra, a few houses down from the Gestapo headquarters. It was a fourth floor apartment in a four-story building. In addition to our small family of three, two other Jewish families would be hiding with us: a childless couple and a family like ours with one daughter, Judka, who was about seven years old like I was. Judka and I were compatible, which was very fortunate because we remained hidden in the apartment without going outdoors for seven long months.

One of my father's fur suppliers had helped make the arrangements for our hiding place with his sister, Aranka. She was an unwed mother, which was a terrible stigma in those days, and she desperately needed money to pay off her debts. Her little son, Cuci, was an adorable child of about three. He was very loveable and well-behaved. We later learned that little Cuci grew up to become a big, tall policeman in Nitra. Unfortunately, his mother proved to be unstable and unreliable. Still, while her motivation for sheltering three Jewish families was far from altruistic, she saved our lives and for this we remain eternally grateful.

The apartment was spacious with two large rooms – one was the living room that included a kitchen, dining area and a large pantry. We were to live here and never leave the premises. In the living room was a hide-a-bed that my mother and I shared. My father slept in the same room on fur pelts laid out on the floor. I don't remember the sleeping arrangements of our fellow "inmates," but I do know that we coalesced as one when confronted by Aranka's violent outbursts. Nothing satisfied Aranka. She flew into rages over trifles and always wanted more money.

As part of the arrangement for our accommodations, my father kept busy during the day working and blocking furs with his business associate. The women sewed, finishing the linings of fur coats, and prepared food. Judka and I played with toys we'd made. I remember a doll I fashioned out of a handkerchief. We played for hours with cut-outs we designed ourselves. We felt innocently secure, Judka and I, protected from harm by our parents during this stressful time.

My father took it upon himself to give Judka and me regular

Hebrew lessons. Although he wasn't the most patient teacher, it was important under the circumstances to structure our time. I also recall how we all huddled quietly around the radio, with the volume turned low so as not to be heard by our neighbours. We listened to the forbidden British Broadcasting Corporation's (BBC) broadcasts, which began with the familiar strains of Beethoven's Fifth Symphony. The airwaves brought us much-needed encouraging news about the Allied advances on the Germans. Such good news was never reported on the local stations, which were censored and full of lies, Nazi propaganda and fabricated German victories.

As I've said, for seven months we never left the apartment. Although the end of the war was near, the Germans, incredibly and obsessively, were still hunting for Jews. We didn't even wear shoes in order to avoid making noise that the tenants below might hear. We would gather around an open window at night in our stocking feet, with the lights off, to get a breath of fresh air.

Aranka's brother helped by bringing us groceries and provisions. But he was not our only visitor. Aranka dated German soldiers and, on several occasions, brought them back to the house. She was totally irresponsible and threw caution to the wind. One of the Jewish women living in hiding acted as her maid and cook, serving Aranka and her German boyfriends cocktails and dinner, while the rest of us huddled in the large pantry. I remember how terrified we all were when I once sneezed, afraid that her German boyfriend would overhear. She would lord it over us, threatening to denounce us, demanding more and more money. "Unless you pay more, I'll go to the SS!" she would shout. My father, not one to be intimidated, would point out, "If you do, you'll be signing your own death-warrant for sheltering Jews." My father stood up to her, but we never knew what to expect. She was totally unpredictable. One morning she was furious because I hadn't greeted her. She upbraided me in front of everyone, shouting about how rude and impolite I was. I was frightened and humiliated.

As the war raged around us, we heard on the BBC that the

Germans were losing ground and in retreat. We were overjoyed. One would have thought that the Germans would concentrate their efforts on ways to shore up their strength. Instead, they continued to obsess about annihilating Jews. They went door to door, searching houses for hidden Jews, Jews who had gotten away. They searched our apartment building and went as far as the third floor.

A widow whose late husband was Jewish lived on the third floor apartment, located directly below ours. She knew about our presence upstairs and was sympathetic to our situation. After the SS searched her home, she said casually, "Don't bother going upstairs. There's nobody there." Fortunately, the SS listened to her and didn't search any further. That was a narrow escape. The kind widow had risked her life and saved ours.

At the end of March 1945, the bloody conflict of war exploded in Slovakia as the Soviet Red Army pushed its way toward Vienna to attack German strongholds. Sirens blared in Nitra, warning the population to take shelter as a blitz of Soviet bombs fell all around. Airplanes carrying their deadly cargo shrieked above us, but we had nowhere to take cover. During the bombings we were afraid to flee; as Jews, we had to remain hidden. But at the same time, it was too dangerous to remain in the apartment. So we realized that the time had come to abandon our hiding place. We were terrified that we would be identified as Jews, but we had no choice. We dressed as unobtrusively as we could and left the apartment, never to return.

People streamed out of Nitra, carrying what they could, searching for shelter from the bombs that were mainly directed at urban areas. We were a mass of moving humanity. Jews and gentiles alike ran for their lives, travelling on foot in the direction of Mount Zobor.

My father was understandably nervous that we would be spotted and singled out as Jews. I remember that I wore a blue kerchief and he shouted at me, "Take that off! Don't you know blue is a Jewish colour?" How paranoid one could become under stress.

We trudged all day, trying to escape the bombardments and devastation that had enveloped Nitra. Houses and buildings lay in ruins all around us. Explosions and the sounds of gunfire and sirens accompanied us. We three fugitive families stayed together on this long and painful trek that led us to the mountain. As night fell, we found a deserted cave. Damp and cold as it was, it had to do as our shelter. I slept on my mother's lap all through that long night. Grateful for her love and protection, I still recall her selfless, tender loving care and self-sacrifice. I knew how uncomfortable she must have been and how little sleep she got in that God-forsaken place.

In the morning, we continued our long and difficult journey, although we didn't know our destination. All we knew was that we were fugitives trying to stay alive, avoiding the bombs falling around us and hoping we wouldn't be shot by the Germans. Suddenly, deep in the forest, we came upon a large, wooden building that we soon realized was a monastery. There, on the mountain, in the middle of the forest, we had come upon the Zobor monastery, a potential safe haven. We were bone-tired and in desperate need of shelter, food and respite. What kind of reception would we get?

We knocked on the large front door. A monk in a long, brown cassock appeared at the entrance. When he saw our dishevelled and exhausted appearance, he kindly let us in. He must have realized immediately that we were Jews on the run. He ushered us upstairs into a large, comfortable room with enough beds for all of us. He explained that because we were Jews, he would allow us the privacy of these quarters. Apparently, there were also many non-Jewish refugees from Nitra on the large ground floor of the monastery. We gratefully lay down to rest, relieved to have been given sanctuary.

No sooner did we begin to relax than there was a sharp knock on the door. To our horror, we saw German officers standing in the doorway, demanding our identity. "These people have been *ausgebombt* (bombed out)," explained the humane and courageous monk accompanying the Germans. Then he gently closed the door. Once again, our lives had been spared. We shall forever be grateful to these deeply religious, righteous monks who showed us compassion and kindness and risked their lives to give us refuge.

In the days that followed, we joined the other refugees for meals in the large common room down below. We blended in with the other Nitra inhabitants, anxiously awaiting the outcome of the bloody battles that raged around us. We knew that the Soviet troops were driving the German forces out of Slovakia but still we wondered: When would the war be over? What would be the outcome for us? To pass the time, we went outside to exercise in the large grassy yard of the monastery. This spacious area was surrounded by a tall, wooden fence with a huge gate that was tightly shut. We milled around, walking up and down the perimeter of the grounds, breathing in the fresh mountain air.

I shall never forget the day, April 4, 1945, when we heard the huge monastery garden gate open wide. We stood perfectly still as victorious Soviet soldiers marched in, liberating us. We were ecstatic. The war was over and the Soviet soldiers were our heroes. We embraced and kissed them and each other, jumping up and down, shouting, laughing and crying. The war was over! We were free. After all these years of terror, fear, madness – the war was finally over.

The Soviet soldiers seemed so friendly and even glamorous to me. I recall a humorous "ransom" they confiscated from us. The soldiers had very little and had gone through terrible deprivation during the war. Of all things, they particularly liked wristwatches. "Casi?" they would ask us. Watch? They would then take our watches and put them on their own wrists, proudly displaying them along with the many other timepieces they had already collected. We gave them our watches gladly, a small price to pay to what seemed to me at the time our cheerful and good-natured liberators.

After the War

By May 1945, although the war was officially over, the difficult task of finding family members and picking up the pieces of our lives still lay ahead. The first thing my parents did was to return to Vráble, where they planned to wait for my grandparents, hoping against hope that they would return.

We remained briefly in Vráble. My parents enrolled me in the local school where I attended kindergarten. This was a bitterly unhappy time for me. The teacher was mean-spirited and antisemitic. She repeatedly picked on me and pulled my ear. I would come home in tears. Finally, my mother went to speak to the principal to complain. The teacher's treatment improved, but I was glad when we decided to leave Vráble for Nitra. When no other Jews returned to Vráble, we accepted the worst. My mother was devastated. Her dear sister, Hedi, with her darling little daughter, Juditka, never returned to Nové Zámky, where she had lived with her husband, Jani, before the war. Jani had survived but was heartbroken without his family. He eventually immigrated to South America and remarried, but we later learned that he tragically took his own life sometime after. We never learned the full story of what had happened in Auschwitz to my grandparents, to Hedi or to Juditka.

While my mother and I waited in Vráble, my father travelled to Nitra and Brno. During that time, my mother lived on unrealized hope. Marka, our maid before the war, remained as loyal as always. She had buried my grandparents' sterling-silver cutlery and other valuables before they were rounded up, keeping them safe, and showed us where they were hidden. One afternoon she took me on an outing to a neighbouring town to visit a friend of our family, an unmarried Hungarian teacher named Piri. Piri's father had been my grandfather's notary and lawyer and our family trusted him. I recall how Piri told Marka that my family ought to be very grateful for all he had done for us during the war, although precisely what it was that he did was not made clear to me. I felt uncomfortable and was glad when we left. I remember walking home hand-in-hand with Marka over the sun-dappled country fields on that beautiful, balmy day, dispelling the dread and unease I had felt during our visit.

By the end of the summer, when all hope of finding missing relatives was lost, we left Vráble. My father sold my grandparents' home and we temporarily moved to Nitra to live at my cousin Nandor's house. It was a large single-family dwelling in the elegant section of town. He had lost his wife in Auschwitz and was living with his daughter who was seven years old, like me. Curiously we both had the same first and last names: we were both named Eva Felsenburgova ("ova" being a common feminine ending for Slavic surnames).

While my father was trying to settle our affairs in Brno, my mother and I stayed on in Nitra and Eva and I were enrolled in the local school. I remember the confusion our identical names caused, as we were both in the same class. I also recall that we were taught the Catholic religion daily and for homework had to memorize passages from the New Testament. The priests who taught religion were very kind to us, giving us pretty pictures of Jesus, Mary and Joseph, which upset our families. Nandor must have spoken to the school authorities because Eva and I were soon excused during the teaching of catechism. We sat in the corridor during these lessons feeling awkward for being singled out. However, the priests were always unfailingly kind to us, even after we were excused from their classes.

My father's cousin Nandor began dating a lovely widow whose husband had been a doctor in Nitra. He and their only son had perished in the Holocaust. The woman was a pharmacist by profession and somehow she survived. They were both lonely and it was only natural that they eventually married.

My cousin Eva, understandably perhaps, was a depressed and unhappy child. My mother tried her best to lavish affection and attention on her, but she sorely missed her mother. Her father bought her expensive presents to try to compensate. Once she received a beautiful doll that opened and closed its eyes, something I had always wanted. My father only brought me a stuffed, plush doll. I was disappointed and jealous, but deep down I realized that I had my beloved mother, whereas she had lost hers.

Eva and I were both sent to a Zionist winter camp in the Slovakian Alps. It was amazing that so soon after the war an organization for Jewish youth, Hashomer Hatzair, was able to gather up the surviving children. I loved this experience. We learned Hebrew Zionist songs and I felt very happy in this friendly and warm atmosphere. Even Eva opened up somewhat. The only discomfort I recall was caused by the poor indoor plumbing. We waited in long lineups to use the bathroom but we joked and teased each other to make the time pass with fun and laughter.

We moved back to Brno in time for the next school term. My father had managed to reclaim our apartment and began the difficult task of rebuilding his business. It had seriously dwindled in his long absence – the war had ruined both the economy and the city. Many buildings and houses in Brno lay in ruins and had to be rebuilt. Others, still standing, had pock-marked damage to the exterior walls from the bombings. We were lucky that our building had remained relatively unharmed. A massive reconstruction began and Brno slowly regained its normalcy.

My mother invited Marka to accompany us back to Brno and stay with us. I was delighted that she accepted. My mother often said,

"One Marka is worth all the modern appliances." She helped with the chores, the cooking and cleaning. She was part of the family but always called my mother "Moje Milospani" (my lady). This formality was the custom at the time in Europe. She had a deep respect and affection for my mother. For me she had another nickname: "Andelcek z roski" (a little angel with horns) because I could be quite mischievous with her, knowing that she almost always let me get away with all my childish pranks.

I was enrolled in the neighbourhood public school in Brno and my first year was challenging. Having gone to the Slovak primary school in Nitra, I was taught the Slovak language and grammar. Although the Czech and Slovak languages are very similar and Slovak speakers easily understand Czechs and vice versa, there are distinct differences in grammar, pronunciation and even vocabulary. Somehow I survived that first year. School began at 8:00 a.m. and went until noon; after lunch it continued from 1:30 to 4:30 p.m. We went home for lunch, so I was able to touch base with my mother or Marka and then return for the afternoon session.

My mother always encouraged me in my studies. To help me in my fluency she spoke to me only in Czech and my father followed suit. Nevertheless, they conversed with each other in Hungarian since it was their mother tongue. Because I heard Hungarian all my life, I can still speak and understand this difficult language, even better than I can Czech or Slovak, which, after immigrating to Canada, I didn't hear often.

The following year in Brno was a very happy one for me, mainly because I was in Mrs. Helena Čechova's class. She was a wonderful teacher and all her students loved her. She made learning fun. In addition to teaching subjects such as Russian, which was now compulsory, she was also our music and art specialist. As hard to believe as this may seem, she made school so entertaining that we were all sorry when 4:30 came and we had to leave. By then I had learned Czech and was more fluent in expressing myself, which helped me in making friends.

I was the only Jewish child in the whole school. My new friend Eva Rientova had a Jewish mother, but her father was a non-Jewish German who had risked his life to protect his family during the war. Eva didn't consider herself, nor her family, Jewish. We became best friends and I often went to her house. We played together after school on Brno Mountain (which we called Spielberg Mountain) and the many parks nearby. Like most children in Brno, we both had scooters – bikes were an extravagance in those days. Those scooters proved to be our favourite means of transportation for the many excursions we made throughout Brno.

Another friend I really liked and looked up to was Kaja Mudrakova. She was the best student in the class and Mrs. Čechova seated me next to her. I later learned she became a doctor. Her father was a barber and she had an older sister who wasn't as talented as she. I remember being invited to her birthday party and how kind she always was to me. There was also Milada Drobna, the class beauty. Pernica, a tall boy in our grade, had a crush on her.

At lunchtime and after school we would skip or play hopscotch and ball in the church yard next to the school. We also played hide-and-seek, only it was not called that. Instead, the children would say, "Let's play 'The Jew is coming,'" whereupon everyone hid except for "the Jew" who had to look for the out-of-sight children. These kinds of accepted antisemitic slurs permeated the atmosphere in pre- and post-war Czechoslovakia.

I also joined the Sokol, the Czech equivalent of the YMCA. We exercised by playing volleyball but were expected to line up quietly when the whistle blew. On one occasion we were more rambunctious than usual. Our instructor asked, "What kind of behaviour is this? You're almost as bad as a Jewish school!" I was a minority of one and felt very sensitive to these put-downs. The general population, how-ever, was born and bred with this kind of prejudice.

In the middle of the school term our class received a new pupil named Peter Sagher from pre-state Israel. I was no longer the only

Jewish child in the school. His father had immigrated to Palestine before the war but had returned to his homeland, Czechoslovakia. As children sometimes are, Peter and I were alternately friends and enemies. We both belonged to Brno's Hashomer Hatzair, the Zionist youth group, which met for after-school activities, holidays and even for a Purim costume party. In later years, I learned that Peter became a doctor, married a Czech woman, and remained in Brno.

For the high holidays – the important fall holidays that extend from the Jewish New Year (Rosh Hashanah) to the Day of Atonement (Yom Kippur) – all the Jewish families celebrated at a large, state-supported synagogue. I enjoyed being there with the people we had come to know in Brno, survivors all. It was a very *heymish*, a comforting, atmosphere. Although most of our families were assimilated and had no religious practice following the war, we observed the holidays and had a strong Jewish identity. Unfortunately, when my husband and I went to Brno in 1987, I could not locate the building. When I inquired at the tourist office about the location of the synagogue, the clerk asked wide-eyed, "What is a synagogue?" It seemed to me that all traces of our community in Brno had sadly been erased.

Ironically, the post-war period in Brno was the happiest and most stable time of my young life. I had been fortunate. Both my parents had been spared and as much as possible we tried to reunite with the remaining members of our family: aunts, uncles and cousins. They visited us and we visited them. We travelled to Budapest and my mother and I stayed with Miriam néni who had survived with her two sons. I recall visiting my aunt Irén, my father's sister, in Budapest, with her two mischievous teenage sons, Pityu and Lalli. My paternal grandfather, who had also survived, lived with them.

On one occasion, I was invited to spend the night at my aunt Marta's house with my cousins Erika and Gyorgy in Budapest. They were older than I was, but aunt Marta wanted to be hospitable. My night fears did not allow me to fall asleep. My uncle Aladar had to take me back to my mother at Miriam néni's house in the middle of the night. I felt like such a baby. I was ashamed to face the girls and the rest of the family the following day, but my mother never held it against me. She always showed boundless compassionate love and understanding of my fears and insecurities.

Nevertheless, I began to grow a little more independent. I travelled to Banska Bystrica with my father's first cousin, Sida Seltzer. She had two sons, Pista and Peter, and invited me to visit them. I had a wonderful and uproarious time with my mischievous cousins. They were always getting into trouble and their mother, who was very strict, was constantly yelling at them. I found it amusing, especially since I was not the subject of her wrath.

The relatively sheltered and carefree life I led in Brno continued in the summer vacations we spent in the countryside. Two summers were especially memorable – the first we spent in Pavlov, a small village in the central Bohemian region not far from Prague, and the following one, in 1948, in Koněšín, in the Harvikovické Highlands about sixty kilometres west of Brno. Two families joined us on these holidays, the Kadlec family and the Hanaks. The Hanak family, who weren't Jewish, had two sons, Rudy and Karl, who were slightly older than I was. My father struck up a friendship with Mr. Hanak that continued by correspondence even after we left Czechoslovakia. During this period my father tried to assimilate into Czech society while keeping his Jewish identity; even my mother, who had come from a strictly Orthodox home, changed. She no longer kept the two sets of dishes prescribed by the kosher dietary laws – one for milk and one for meat. It was now impossible to get kosher meat, so we ate *treif* (non-kosher food), but we never had pork in the house. Later, in Canada, where kosher food was available, my mother returned to buying only kosher meat.

I had great fun during these delightful summers. I was free from school and because my father had to attend to business in Brno, I had my beloved mother to myself. I loved being in the tranquil countryside. In Pavlov I made friends with a peasant girl, a neighbour with whom I would play with dolls and toys for hours on end. We whiled away the time under an old sheltering tree whose trunk and branches offered endless possibilities to the imagination. We ran and played in the open fields as my mother indulged in her love of reading. My father's visits, however, were stressful. He would arrive by bus for the weekend, tired and nervous after his fifty-kilometre trip from Brno. Once, a friend gave him a lift on his motorcycle. Cars were scarce and motorcycles were a popular means of transportation. Speeding up and down the steep mountain roads was nevertheless more than my father had bargained for. I remember him describing his voyage more than once. "We were three of us travelling on a single motorcycle," he explained. "The third was the good Lord, who took care of us."

Rudy, Karl and I had fun swimming in the small river that ran through Pavlov. In those days there were no concerns about pollution. We jumped off a small bridge into the cool water and swam right through the middle of the quiet town.

The following summer, in Koněšín, we rented a room in a large farmhouse. This time, along with the Hanak boys, little Jiři Kadlec was my frequent companion. We received room and board and I recall my mother worrying that the dishes were not clean enough. The tenants used to pitch in with the clean-up after meals but my mother took over the dish-washing to ensure good hygiene.

My cousin Eva came from Nitra to stay with us for two weeks when her father and his new wife went on their honeymoon. She brought chocolate bars – a rare luxury at the time. My mother doled out these sweets very sparingly so as to conserve and savour the special treat.

I was ten years old when Karl, the older of the two Hanak boys, informed me about the birds and the bees and the way that babies were conceived. How naive and innocent we were in those days! I didn't believe him and thought he was being ridiculous. Actually, he was my first "boyfriend." He complimented me on my appearance and was very attentive to me. His younger brother, Rudy, not much of a ladies' man, tried to imitate his older brother by paying court to Eva. There was a large barn in the farmyard that was filled with hay. The four of us would climb up to the loft on a tall ladder and jump down onto the bales of hay. What carefree fun! Together with our parents, we also trekked a long way through wheat fields to reach the lake where we picnicked, swam and built sand castles.

This was an idyllic time, except for the fearful nights. After the children had been put to bed, the adults would gather to play cards. At night, as I lay alone in bed, the sounds of the barking dogs of Koněšín terrified me. I dreaded the dark and those sharp, menacing barks. Although I was a big girl of ten, my mother would stay with me, tenderly holding my hand until I drifted off to sleep, assuring me that she didn't like card games. My mother saved my life emotionally. She was always there for me with tender loving care, attention and her physical presence.

Leaving Europe

In the years immediately after the war, our life in Brno continued in a busy and, as far as I was concerned, enjoyable way. On Sundays during the school year we often went on excursions outside the city, taking the local train to the countryside. We would go on this *vilet* (outing) with several other families and their children. Except for our neighbour, Gerti Kadlec, our companions weren't Jewish, but were kind and good people with whom we later remained in contact through letters. I remember in particular the Komarek family. They had a very lovely daughter who was in her twenties at the time. She had a Jewish boyfriend, a young man somewhat older than she and very good-looking. Although she was in love with him, her parents were skeptical: "He will never marry her. Jews stick to their own kind." Their words proved to be true. For whatever reason, they eventually broke up.

We took full advantage of the rich cultural life that resumed in Brno after the war. We went to the theatre, to puppet shows and to the opera – which I hated because I couldn't understand the words and it seemed so long and boring. I also took piano lessons and my mother took me swimming at Brno's public beach. I remember doing laps as she watched. She would bring sandwiches and snacks and I looked forward to these outings.

Although I didn't realize it, Czechoslovakia was in turmoil and events suddenly came to a crisis point on March 10, 1948, with the so-called suicide of Jan Masaryk, the champion of democracy and human rights. The son of Tomáš G. Masaryk, Czechoslovakia's American-educated and beloved first president, Jan Masaryk already had an eminent political career. During World War II he had been foreign minister in the Czech government-in-exile in Great Britain headed by Edvard Beneš. He supported a policy of cooperation with the Soviet Union as well as with the Western powers. Masaryk continued to hold his post after his government returned to Prague in 1945 and remained in office after the Communist coup d'état in February 1948. That March, barely a month later, Jan Masryk was found dead in the courtyard of his home. Officially declared a suicide, it was evident that Masaryk, who had everything to live for, had been pushed out of his window to his death. For us, his death signalled more upheaval and insecurity.

Soon after, the Communist Party, with backing from Moscow, took control of the Czech government with disastrous results. All privately owned businesses were seized and "nationalized." My father's considerable efforts to get back on his feet economically came to naught. My parents lost everything – everything they had was confiscated by the strong-arm tactics of the Communist government.

That was the last straw. My father wanted out. But where to go? The new State of Israel beckoned all Jewish refugees with open arms and my parents decided to leave for our spiritual homeland. Still, they were worried. How would a furrier earn a living in a hot climate and in an economically strained new state? My father would have a tough time making a livelihood in Israel. Nevertheless, they packed up our worldly possessions in a "lift" (a large wooden crate the size of a small room), including our piano, my father's bicycle and all our furniture, and dispatched it to Eretz Yisrael, the Land of Israel.

At the very last moment, however, my parents changed their plans. My aunt Hedvig, my father's oldest sister, had survived Auschwitz and, as a displaced person, had been admitted to Canada. At the eleventh hour, she sponsored us, mailing us an affidavit that legally permitted us to come to this land of ice and snow – a much more promising place for my father to earn his living in the fur business, the only trade he knew. My parents gave my mother's cousin Willy, who lived in Tel Aviv, all our possessions – it didn't pay to ship the lift to Canada. The price of the delivery would exceed the value of the contents. In October 1949, we left Czechoslovakia with nothing and set off for the great white north.

~

We journeyed first by train to the port of Le Havre, France, where we boarded the SS *Samaria*, a passenger liner. The *Samaria* was a beautiful ship, with dark wood panelling and fine copper fittings. We, however, were in second class. My mother and I shared a cabin and my father was in another part of the ship with the male refugees. All I remember about our ocean voyage across the stormy October Atlantic was that it was terrifying and terrible. I never thought we'd make it. Waves as high as mountains tossed our boat to and fro like a plaything. Because of the stormy weather we wore life jackets most of the time. I was desperately seasick. I had my twelfth birthday on the ship. For a present all I asked for was a dozen oranges, something we could neither obtain nor afford in post-war Czechoslovakia. Mostly, however, I spent my time in bed in our tiny cabin, which creaked and heaved. When we did manage to visit the splendid dining room, outfitted with beautiful chandeliers and opulent velvet-upholstered chairs, the furniture slid from one end of the room to the other. It was impossible to sit down to a meal even if we had wanted to.

We were at sea for ten days. I couldn't believe it when, two days after we were scheduled to arrive, we finally saw land. In no time, we'd made it to Quebec City! We all cheered when we saw in the far distance the Plains of Abraham, bringing us closer to what would be our new home.

When the SS *Samaria* finally docked in Quebec City's harbour, we were ushered into a huge holding area. Waiting for us, and for the few other Jewish families on board, were ladies from the Jewish Immigrant Aid Society (JIAS) with sandwiches, hot drinks and fruit. I tasted my first banana at this welcoming reception on Canadian soil.

After a brief stopover in the bitterly cold Quebec City (a place well-suited for fur apparel), we boarded the train for the four-hour ride to Montreal. Looking out the window of our speeding coach, I saw the flat, frozen landscape hurtling past and was filled with anticipation. After the war in Czechoslovakia I had loved going to see Hollywood films and had visions of North America filled with glamorous, dream-like images from the movies that I so enjoyed. *National Velvet* with Elizabeth Taylor, *The Adventures of Robin Hood* with Errol Flynn and Olivia de Havilland, and the hilarious films of Charlie Chaplin, such as *The Great Dictator*, were some of my favourites. My classmates back in Czechoslovakia all envied me because I was moving to the magical continent of figure-skating champion Sonja Henie and the adorable Shirley Temple. I fully expected the streets of Montreal to resemble Hollywood movie sets.

How disappointed I was upon our arrival in Montreal, the city that would be my home for the rest of my life! In the dead of winter, Montreal was freezing and inhospitable.

We arrived exhausted and uncertain of our future. What kind of life lay ahead? How would we manage?

My father considered us lucky because for the first few days his friend, Mr. Vladar, shared his family's flat on Clark Street with us. It was the farthest thing imaginable from Hollywood. Wooden, ladder-like stairs covered with ice and snow coiled up the three-story triplex. The house seemed small, dim, old-fashioned. Luckily, we only stayed there for a few days.

Aunt Hedvig had rented two rooms for us from a kindly Jewish couple, Mr. and Mrs. Holtzman, who lived in a spacious flat on Hutchison Street. Their two children were married, so they had plenty of room. This was a very wise choice for us because the Holtzmans helped us learn, almost through osmosis, the Canadian Jewish way of life.

Their home was beautifully appointed, with elegant furniture. My parents were to have the bedroom facing the street that had belonged to their daughter, Maisie. My room, at the other end of the flat, had probably been the maid's room, although it certainly was good enough for me. It had a bed and dresser, as well as a card table that served as my desk. Down the hall from my room were stairs to the "shed" – a ground-floor storage space. At night an army of mice came up from the shed and danced under my bed. I remember the scratching and scurrying noises they made in the middle of the night.

In spite of the nightly rodent visits, I was comfortable in our new home. The Holtzmans were kind and hospitable. When my parents returned from work, the Holtzmans made sure to vacate the kitchen and give us privacy. They even included us in their large, extended family for holiday celebrations. At one of the grand holiday meals in the Holtzmans' large dining room I remember sitting next to Mrs. Holtzman's brother, who was a lawyer. He told me that I had an "English complexion." I treasured his compliment.

Many challenges awaited me in my new homeland. Chief among them was attending school and integrating with my new classmates. A few days after we settled into our home on Hutchison Street, my mother and I walked to Alfred Joyce School, around the corner from where we lived. We entered through the large front gates and made our way to the principal's office where Mr. Samson, a distinguished gentleman, sized us up as non-English speakers. He immediately called for an interpreter. Mona, a seventh-grade student with blond hair, blue eyes and a friendly smile appeared at the office to dutifully translate Mr. Samson's rudimentary questions into Yiddish: "What is your name?" "How old are you?" "Where do you live?" he asked. We didn't speak Yiddish and these questions were easy enough even for me to understand in English. Still, we went along with Mona's careful Yiddish version.

The Grade 5 class to which I was relegated was entirely populated by girls; there were no mixed classes in the school. My teacher, Miss Langmour, and her pupils were most welcoming and friendly. In fact, my lifelong friend, Marilyn Feldstein, was a classmate who conveniently lived a few houses up from me on Hutchison Street. When I graduated to Grade 6, my teacher, Mrs. McKenzie, a no-nonsense, strict but fair lady, recommended that I skip a grade and go straight into high school. Although this encouraged me, when I arrived at the large and very impersonal Strathcona Academy, I felt bewildered and isolated. Even worse, there was no lunchroom and I had to make the long trek home at noon to eat lunch and then back again in the afternoon. I was often sick with the flu that year – a cold education in every sense of the word.

In those first few years our landlady, Mrs. Holtzman, was particularly warm, kind and considerate to me. Both my parents worked long hours in fur factories – difficult, manual labour to which neither was accustomed – and I was often left alone. One day, Mrs. Holtzman treated me to lunch at the elegant restaurant on Eaton's ninth floor and after lunch we went to see the Walt Disney animated movie *Cinderella*. To this day I recall that wonderful day with our thoughtful landlady. I remember being shocked to learn that Mrs. Holtzman could neither read nor write. She was so clever and refined that I never guessed she was unlettered – except that she would ask me to read her the letters from her daughter, Maisie, who lived in Yarmouth, Nova Scotia. Too ashamed that she could not read, she told me that she had poor eyesight.

Life wasn't easy, especially for my parents. No longer young (my mother was forty-two and my father fifty-four when we arrived in Canada), they were forced to seek employment wherever it was available. My father stood all day as he blocked and stretched fur pelts and skins on a large table. He hammered nails into the edge of the furs, stretching them as large and flat as possible. He would come home with terrible pains in his legs and feet every evening. My mother worked as a finisher in a fur factory, sewing linings into fur coats. After a long day's work she would stop to pick up groceries, prepare supper, make sandwiches for lunch for the three of us for the following day, wash dishes and still have time to dictate my spelling homework.

I worried about my parents. I waited for them on those dark, winter nights when they were late coming home. I remember heating up their slippers by putting them under the radiators so that when they arrived, they would feel warmth and comfort. My poor mother lost most of her hair during that time, probably due to stress. In later years, her hair grew back a beautiful silver grey. In spite of the stress and strain that both my parents suffered, they loved Canada fiercely. "I always loved it here," was a refrain I heard my mother say over and over again. Knowing how hard life was for her, I would ask, "Why do you love Canada so much?" "Freedom! Democracy! And independence!" was her reply. She would add, with a smile, "I loved earning my own money."

Life's Journey

My parents worked hard to build a life for us in Canada. My father was a very enterprising person who found it extremely difficult to work for someone else in a factory. Determined to establish a business venture on his own, he joined a Czech tailor, Mr. Janovic, who had a repair and remodelling shop on Bernard Avenue. My father rented half the shop to repair and remodel fur coats. After building up his own loyal clientele, my father moved into his own place on Laurier Avenue – this was before it became a fashionable street. My mother, too, longed for a place of her own. In 1954, after five years of living with the Holtzmans, my parents decided to rent their own duplex apartment on de la Peltrie Street.

The rent made it difficult for my parents to make ends meet, so my father gave up the shop and worked out of our basement, seeing customers by appointment upstairs. My mother quit her factory work and began working full-time for my father at home, fitting and finishing the linings of fur coats. They both put in long hours of labour, but they were very grateful. They had their own small business and, above all, they were independent, without a boss to answer to. This independence was very precious to them.

There were two hectic times of year when business was extremely busy: before winter set in, when clients arrived with their fur coats, jackets and stoles for repairs or remodelling; and after the cold winter season, when my parents arranged for coats to be stored. My parents had a variety of clients – French-Canadian, English Protestant and Jewish. They would set up appointments for try-ons and fittings and estimate the cost of work to be done. My father was good at public relations and making polite small talk. I remember how clients would stand in front of the hall mirror as my parents adjusted the coats for fittings. Of course, the greatest margin of profit came if a client ordered a brand-new coat, although these orders were rare. During these busy times of the year I kept out of the way, confined to my room or the kitchen. The business visits did not interfere with my life, but I felt the strain and pressure as my parents worked so hard to meet deadlines during "the season." After winter, my father would phone all his customers and personally pick up their fur coats to be put in the storage facility. Since we had no car, he visited his clients by foot, bus or streetcar, carrying their garments in large, plastic bags. When winter approached, he delivered them back.

There was one particular customer, Miss Martineau, with whom my parents were very friendly. At Christmas she would arrive at the house with thoughtful gifts, even something for me. I remember the beautifully wrapped dolls and trinkets that she brought to our house. One day, however, she said something that greatly upset my father. He had commented that one should not judge people or nations as a whole, but rather consider individuals on their own merit. Ignorant of our background, Miss Martineau responded, "Well, except for the Jews. They're evil and each one of them is not to be trusted." My father was too shocked to reply, so he said nothing. When Miss Martineau left, he asked me to write her a letter. By now my English had much improved. In the note he explained that he could no longer work for her because he, too, was a Jew. He ended the letter with a very strong statement that I still vividly recall: "I'd like to remind you that Jesus Christ was also a Jew." Miss Martineau actually apologized and continued to use my father as her furrier, as did her family.

Although we were settling into Canadian life, there were still incidents that harkened back to our past. On weekends we would take long walks down the neighbouring streets. Park Avenue was a popular destination where we often bumped into people we knew, other immigrants out for a stroll. My father wore a long, leather coat, as was the European fashion at the time. One Saturday, a man – obviously a concentration camp survivor and very distraught – accosted my tall, blue-eyed, fair-haired father, shouting angrily, "I recognize you from the camp! You were an SS officer and I will denounce you!" We were taken aback. My father, never at a loss, shot back, "I'm a dirty Jew, just like you." Such stereotypes of ourselves were the baggage most survivors carried. We were alternately ashamed and proud of being Jewish. We had a heightened sensitivity to any comment or appearance of antisemitism. We shared feelings of inferiority and insecurity about our identity. We felt vulnerable, different and apart, yet proud of Jews and of Israel. Being Jewish always coloured our perceptions.

As for me, I concentrated all my efforts on my studies. I had a strong desire to succeed academically. I was a "social hybrid," with one foot in my European roots and the other, very insecurely, in my new homeland. I felt lost and uncomfortable so I plunged into my studies. My mother never wanted me to help with any household chores, encouraging me instead to do my schoolwork. She would often ask gently, "Did you finish your homework?" This used to irritate me, but she nevertheless spurred me on to focus on my studies.

When we moved from Hutchison to de la Peltrie Street, I switched over to the Montreal High School for Girls. My favourite subjects were English literature and composition. I especially liked North American literature, inspired by my wonderful teacher, Miss Barrington. Later, in Grade 10, after having been in Canada for four years, I wrote an essay that expressed my nostalgia for a time and place I had known and fondly remembered: Brno (at the time I called it "Brunn" by its international, German name). My Grade 10 teacher, Miss Hutchison, read it to the class, which made me very proud. My essay, entitled "Memories," described Brno's attributes – its outdoor markets, graceful streets, parks and squares, its stately architecture, the Spielberg Castle, the bustling railway station and my fond memories of my school and fellow students. I concluded my essay with the following words:

Next year I shall become a Canadian citizen. I have made new friends, and learned to love and appreciate Canada and the things she has to offer. Yet I shall never forget Brunn.

Of course, there is much more that I shall never forget and that I did not express in my high school composition. Now, in writing about my wartime experiences, I clearly realize that I shall never forget them. They are an integral part of who I am. Emotions and feelings are intangible reminders.

My parents were so proud at my graduation when I finished first in my class and second in the school. My mother could never fulfill her dream of becoming a teacher and I was gratified that she could vicariously fulfill her wish through me. I went on to MacDonald College for Teachers in Ste. Anne de Bellevue on a scholarship.

During this time, my parents were faced with many obstacles as they struggled to earn a livelihood and become established. In 1955 my father suffered the first of a series of heart attacks. Thankfully, he recovered and carried on with his work and daily routine. A year later, in 1956, life also dealt my mother a terrible blow. One day we were invited to dinner at the Holtzmans' apartment. At the time, I was boarding at the college, about forty kilometres from Montreal. My friend Marilyn had come with me, and we were to meet my parents there. When my parents didn't show up, we began to worry. The terrible phone call came that my mother had been struck down on the road by a speeding car, driven by a drunk driver. She had been taken to St. Mary's Hospital by ambulance.

Marilyn accompanied me to the hospital and we spent the night together with my father – waiting. Seeing my mother's fur coat, torn, and her little hat stained with blood brought me to the point of desperation. She almost died from her injuries. Her pelvis was broken in nine places.

Each weekend I made the trip from MacDonald College to visit my mother. She was suspended in a sling, immobile, so that her bones could fuse and mend. She remained in the sling for six long months without moving. She suffered terribly. She told me many times how she loved the morphine they gave her to relieve the pain. The doctors gradually weaned her off the narcotic so she wouldn't become addicted. When she finally returned home, she had to learn to walk all over again. It took her a long time to be able to lift her legs or go up the stairs to the second floor of the duplex. After she came home from the hospital, my mother also became depressed. No wonder! Her body had been shattered and she could barely move. She cried often, unable to stop the tears. To see her suffering both mentally and physically was very distressing. My father did the best he could to be helpful while I was away at college. He shopped and even cooked until she eventually came out of this sadness. She even willed herself to walk again, doing her exercises for a full hour every day until she could resume her former activities.

∼

In 1957, when I was twenty years old and still studying at MacDonald College I met my husband, Herbert Marx, on a blind date. Two years later, in December 1959, we were married. Both my parents were very fond of Herbert, and he got along extremely well with them. We even vacationed together for many summers on Cape Cod and in the Eastern Townships.

My father died in 1972, at the age of seventy-six, from heart disease. He lived to see his two grandchildren – our son, Robert, who was born in 1965, and our daughter, Sarah, born in 1970. He was a very proud and affectionate *zeidie* (grandfather), a devoted, loyal family man, and honest and straight in all his business and personal dealings. I was not as close to him as I was to my mother and we often disagreed. Despite our clashes and arguments, though, I loved him. As I matured, I was able to rise above our differences and we had a devoted and amicable relationship. He loved travel and when they could finally afford it, he went with my mother to Europe, Israel and across Canada.

Our small family was blessed to have my mother with us until her ninety-fifth year. A widow for thirty-one years, she was an integral part of our nuclear family. She lived on her own after the death of my father, maintaining a charming apartment that was immaculate. She invited us for dinner every Sunday night until, in her late seventies, it became too much for her. "I give back my license," she declared.

My mother went to the Golden Age Association, where she met new friends and took French classes. She continued to study French when she accompanied us to France during my husband's 1977 sabbatical year. We lived in Aix-en-Provence, a beautiful town, where we rented an apartment for ten months. She shared a room with our son, Robbie, who, at the time, was twelve years old. He was preparing for his bar mitzvah to be held in May of that year at the Western Wall in Jerusalem. Diligently, she helped him practice the Torah portion that he would read aloud at his bar mitzvah. Although she was very bored in France that year since we were all busy with various activities and taking courses, she still got along and tried to learn the language. Amazingly, she somehow managed to read all of the Maigret books in the original French and even surprised me on my fortieth birthday by ordering my favourite St. Honoré cake from the local patisserie.

When they were young, my mother helped with the children. She spent many hours by the piano, patiently listening to our daughter, Sarah, practicing her music. In fact, she took part in all of the children's activities with pride. She was also a great help when Robbie became ill. When he was four years old he developed red marks on his arms and legs. Thinking that this was an allergy, I took him to our pediatrician who hospitalized Robbie on the spot. Eventually, our son was diagnosed with idiopathic thrombocytopenic purpura, ITP for short, which means "bleeding under the skin." This was a terrible shock for us. Robbie was put on a high dose of cortisone medication and was not allowed to play in the park or attend nursery school.

At home we covered all sharp edges of the furniture with thick towels and blankets so that Robbie wouldn't injure himself. His face and body swelled as a result of the cortisone treatment. We had to go for weekly platelet counts and his platelets were not increasing. The doctors considered removing his spleen to help improve his condition. I felt desperate and helpless. My mother, meanwhile, had heard of a similar case where a child had been helped by drinking fresh lemon juice daily. I was ready to try anything, so I began squeezing lemon juice for him, adding fresh orange juice and sugar to make it more palatable. When we next went for Robbie's platelet count, it had increased dramatically. Our doctor, who was skeptical of this "cure," suggested that I give Robbie vitamin C pills, or even canned orange juice, to save myself the extra work. None of these substitutes worked. I therefore continued to prepare the lemon juice "cocktail" until gradually his platelets returned to normal. He was able to attend kindergarten that fall. Until he was fourteen he still continued to be tested – and I continued to prepare the cocktail. But I give full credit to my mother's advice for Robbie being able to have a normal childhood and lead a productive adult life.

My mother's health eventually began to fail and on Christmas Eve 2002, I had to call 911. She had moved in with us in 1987 after falling and breaking her hip. While she lay on the stretcher in the ambulance she looked out the windows and said, "I always loved it here," over and over again. She was diagnosed with kidney failure. During the period when she wasn't well, she would not give in. "I'll walk," she would say determinedly. When she was no longer able to walk, she would say, "That's why I have the wheelchair, so I can use it." Although I know that she hated it.

My mother's last days exemplified her courage, determination and self-discipline to the very end. We called my mother the "no-complain lady," always the optimist. Even when she was very unwell, doubled over in discomfort, and we would talk into her ear (because she was hard of hearing) and ask, "How are you?" she would answer, "Very well, thank you." She was unfailingly gracious and polite, even under severely limiting disabilities.

At night she would say her prayers, although she had trouble breathing. Each morning (and even in the middle of the night when she woke up) she would say, "I have to make the salad!" because it had been her job to prepare my husband's vegetables. She brought me to tears many times during the day with her polite "thank you" for each little gesture of kindness or service. Even a pat on the hand or a kiss got a "thank you." She often said, "I always loved you." And about our children, Robbie and Sarah, she said repeatedly, "I was always crazy about them. I loved them as my own. The only thing I didn't do was give birth to them." And when I told her that I loved her, she responded, "I love you, too."

My mother said that she did what the Ten Commandments tell us to do. That was her recipe for being a "good Jewish person." She wore a watch at all times. ("We Jews must always know the time!") "Be nice. And give!" she summed up. My mother has left such a legacy in our hearts.

When I asked her, "Mommy, what hurts you?" She would reply, "Nothing. I'm ninety-three years old" – although by that time she was ninety-five. Ever the realist, she would add, "I'm no baby. That's what hurts me." She often pointed to her head and said, "It works."

On January 18, 2004, however, my mother said, "I don't know where I am. This never happened to me." She broke my heart. She died two days later.

May her memory be for a blessing.

Epilogue

In 1987 I returned to visit Vráble with my husband. We found my grandparents' home still standing with its garden and iron gate, but it was occupied by strangers. We visited with my dearest Marka, which was a very emotional reunion. Although I had not seen her since we left Czechoslovakia in 1949, we continued to correspond with her, sending cash gifts and photos. She also wrote to us regularly, so we kept up to date with each other's news. Sadly, she passed away a few years ago, but we are still in touch with her nephew, Dusan Piesik, and send a generous gift in her blessed memory each Christmas.

My mother's immediate family perished in the Holocaust. My father's family was more fortunate. With the exception of my grieving aunt Hedvig, my father's oldest sister from Debrecen who had lost her husband and older son in Auschwitz, my father's two older brothers and two sisters, their families and my grandfather all survived in Budapest. Perhaps safe houses like those created by Raoul Wallenberg and other courageous diplomats helped to save their lives.

My father's oldest brother, Norbert, a widower, and his son, Pauli, moved to Paris after the war. My father's brother Erno, with his wife, Ilka, and only daughter, Edith, moved to Israel. Although they have all died by now, we are in contact with their granddaughter, Uta, her husband, Yoav, and their three wonderful boys, as well as with Erno's grandson, Elli, his wife and their three daughters. My father's oldest sister, Marta, and her husband, Aladar, moved to New York with their daughters, Erika and Gyorgy. His youngest sister, Blanka, with her husband, Joska, survived with their daughter, Erzsi Kovacs. She is my only remaining relative in Budapest. She married and later divorced a non-Jewish man with whom she had two daughters, one of whom was tragically killed, hit by a car. The younger one, Petra, has two small children, Samu and Lea, with her Hungarian partner. We recently visited them in Budapest, the last remnant of a large, extended family that remain in Hungary.

My father's favourite sister, Iren, a widow, moved to Israel with her two sons, Pityu and Lalli. We keep in touch with Pityu, the older son, and his wife, Ora, whom we visit frequently in Israel along with Lalli's widow, Judith. Lalli was killed tragically in a motorcycle accident in Israel, leaving two children, Esther and Josi, who are raising their families in Israel.

My father's cousin Nandor and his second wife, along with my cousin Eva, also moved to Israel. Their marriage produced a daughter, Tamar, who did not marry. But Eva is now a proud grandmother of six! When she and I meet, we never talk about the past. It must be too painful to bring up hurtful childhood memories.

I lost contact with my father's cousin Sida Seltzer's two sons, Pista and Peter, with whom I had visited in Banska Bystrica. About five years ago, however, I received a letter from Peter, my younger cousin. He and his wife, Julia, were planning to visit North America. Could they see us? I was delighted and we re-established contact. My husband and I even visited him and his brother and their families at their home in Zurich in 2005.

On my mother's side, Miriam néni survived with her two sons. Her son Miklos and his wife converted from Judaism and became Catholics. They said that they were tired of suffering the persecution and prejudice to which Jews are subjected and wanted a fresh start. They moved to Brazil with Miriam néni and her younger son, Imre, and his wife and daughter. Aunt Miriam came twice to visit us in

Canada. She loved my mother and my mother was very fond of her, too.

My mother's uncle Matyi also survived with his wife, Elli. Their only son, Tommy, tragically disappeared during the war without a trace. Most likely he was picked up and deported to a concentration camp, as was the terrifying custom of the SS and their Hungarian collaborators on the prowl in Budapest. This type of anonymous abduction of young people is described in the book *Fatelessness* by the Hungarian Jewish Nobel Prize-winning author Imre Kertész. Tommy had been very gifted and talented. His parents adored him. They never gave up hope that he was alive somewhere, but eventually they had to accept the dreadful truth. They moved to Australia and later, because they were lonely, moved to Brazil, joining Miriam in Sao Paulo. Matyi and Elli also visited us in Canada and brought us two cute stuffed koala bears as a souvenir from their sojourn in Australia.

Uncle Willie and Aunt Wilma Rosenbaum, who were so kind to me during my illness in Budapest during the war, ended up in Australia with their two sons. My mother's cousins Imre and Willy Rosenbaum, both originally from Paks, escaped to Palestine during the war. With my parents' help, Imre (or Joshua Ronn, as he became known in Israel) came to Canada. My mother always refered to him as "my favourite cousin." He and his wife, Lilly, and their two children, Chaim and Naomi, live in Montreal with their families and we see them frequently.

My cousin Tibi Deutsch has not been able to exorcise his bitter experiences. The younger son of my aunt Hedvig, he cannot erase the horrific killing of his brother, who was murdered in front of his eyes, beaten to death by the vicious foreman at a German slave labour camp. Tibi lives in Los Angeles. He is obsessed by these horrific experiences. At age seventy-eight, with the onset of Alzheimer's disease, these memories dominate his conversation and his thinking.

Through all the years, my parents tried to block out the past. They rolled up their sleeves and got on with life. Memories, however, lingered forever. My mother's closest and dearest immediate family perished and she never ceased to mourn their loss. When I was a young girl I remember attending the funeral of an acquaintance with my parents. We hardly knew the deceased but my mother was consumed with paroxysms of grief. When I asked what the matter was, she replied, "I am crying for my parents, my sister, my family. They have no graves."

My parents had a book we called their "bible," to which they frequently referred. When it fell apart, I replaced it with a brand-new copy. It was *The Rise and Fall of the Third Reich* by William L. Shirer, a compelling account of the historical events they had lived through and experienced firsthand. My mother and father read and re-read many parts of the book, reliving, as it were, their wartime experiences. My mother explained, "I have a real pleasure in reading about how the Germans got it!"

I am blessed with a loving, supportive family and four beautiful grandchildren, Ella, Hannah, Harry and David. Yet, no one who has survived the Holocaust has survived unscathed. I owe my life to my parents. They bore the brunt of the suffering and were the true survivors, through whose heroic and courageous efforts I, too, survived. They deserve all the credit for my coming out of the terror alive.

Glossary

Allies The coalition of countries that fought against Germany, Italy and Japan (the Axis nations). At the beginning of World War II in September 1939, the coalition included France, Poland and Britain. Once Germany invaded France in 1940 and the United States entered the war following the bombing of Pearl Harbor by Japan on December 7, 1941, the main leaders of the Allied powers became Britain, the USSR and the United States. Other Allies included Canada, Australia, Czechoslovakia, Greece, Mexico, Brazil, South Africa and China.

Army PX (Post Exchange) Stores with subsidized goods set up by the US government for military personnel posted in foreign countries.

Arrow Cross Party (in Hungarian, *Nyilaskeresztes Párt – Hungarista Mozgalom*; short form: Nyilas). The extreme pro-Nazi fascist and antisemitic party founded in 1935 under the name the Party of National Will and led by Ferenc Szálasi. With the full support of Nazi Germany, the newly renamed Arrow Cross Party ran in Hungary's 1939 election and won 25 per cent of the vote. Despite this, the party's extreme fascist ideology caused it to be excluded from Miklós Horthy's pro-Nazi government. When Horthy announced in October 1944 that Hungary would end its alliance with the Nazis and withdraw from the war, the Germans' response was to support the Arrow Cross Party in a coup d'état and install an Arrow Cross government under Szálasi's leadership. In addition to the thousands of Hungarian Jews who had been deported to Nazi death camps during the Horthy regime, between October 15, 1944 and March 1945 the Arrow Cross instigated the murder of tens of thousands of Hungarian Jews. In one specific incident on November 8, 1944, more than 70,000 Jews were rounded up and sent on a death march to Nazi camps in Austria. The remaining Jewish population of Budapest was forced into a closed ghetto and, between December 1944 and January 1945, approximately 20,000 of them were shot along the banks of the Danube by the Arrow Cross.

Aryan A nineteenth-century anthropological term originally used to refer to the Indo-European family of languages and, by extension, the peoples who spoke them. It became a synonym for people of Nordic or Germanic descent in the theories that inspired Nazi racial ideology. "Aryan" was an official classification in Nazi racial laws to denote someone of pure Germanic blood, as opposed to "non-Aryans," such as Slavs, Jews, part-Jews, Roma and Sinti, and others of supposedly inferior racial stock.

assimilation A term used to refer to the cultural assimilation and social integration of Jews into the surrounding culture. Before the eighteenth century many European countries, including Hungary and Czechoslovakia, restricted where Jewish people could live and excluded them from certain professions, educational opportunities and land ownership. In 1849 new laws in the Austrian Empire permitted free movement for Jews of Bohemia and Moravia, and in 1867 the Jews of Hungary were granted full equality. For many Jews this emancipation resulted in a modernization of Jewish religious and cultural practices, including language, clothing, customs, professions and cultural life.

Auschwitz (German; in Polish, Oświęcim) A town in southern Poland approximately forty kilometres from Krakow, it is also the name of the largest complex of Nazi concentration camps that were built nearby. The Auschwitz complex contained three main camps: Auschwitz I, a slave labour camp built in May 1940; Auschwitz II-Birkenau, a death camp built in early 1942; and Auschwitz-Monowitz, a slave labour camp built in October 1942. In 1941 Auschwitz I was a testing site for usage of the lethal gas Zyklon B as a method of mass killing, which then went into wide usage. The Auschwitz complex was liberated by the Soviet army in January 1945.

Austerlitz, Battle of (also called Battle of the Three Emperors) French battle led by Napoleon Bonaparte against the Russian and Austrian armies on December 2, 1805, in Austerlitz in Moravia, ten kilometres southeast of Brno. France's tactical victory against the army of Tsar Alexander I made the battle one of the most famous of the Napoleonic wars.

Ave Maria (Latin; also known as Hail Mary or the Angelic Salutation) A traditional Catholic prayer asking Mary, the mother of Jesus, to intercede on behalf of the worshipper. Used in both public liturgy and in private worship as part of the Rosary devotions. *See also* Rosary.

ÁVO (in Hungarian, Államvédelmi Osztálya) State Protection Department. A branch of the Soviet secret police that operated in Hungary from 1946 to 1956, the ÁVO was brutally violent and much feared. During the Hungarian Revolution in 1956 rebels sought revenge, killing many of the officers of ÁVO and informants that worked for them.

balebusteh (Yiddish; also balabusteh, balaboostah) A devoted homemaker.

Beneš, Edvard (1884–1948) The second and fourth president of Czechoslovakia (1935–1938 and 1945–1948). After Germany took control of part of Czechoslovakia in 1938, Beneš went into exile in Britain, where he formed the Czechoslovak government-in-exile. After the war, Beneš was reinstated as president until the Communist coup in February 1948; he resigned in June of that year and was succeeded by Communist leader Klement Gottwald.

Bergen-Belsen A concentration camp initially established by the Nazis near Celle, Germany in 1940 for prisoners of war. After 1943, it also held so-called exchange Jews, whom Germany hoped to use in peace negotiations with the Allies. After March 1944, part of the camp was designated as a "recovery camp" and one thousand prisoners from Mittelbau-Dora and other forced labour camps who were too sick to work were sent to Bergen-Belsen. They did not receive any treatment, but instead were left to die from starvation and disease. Toward the end of the war, thousands of prisoners from camps close to the front lines, such as Auschwitz, Mittelbau-Dora and Buchenwald were taken there, primarily on death marches. With the influx of inmates, camp conditions deteriorated rapidly and some 35,000 people died there between January and April 1945. British forces liberated the camp on April 15, 1945.

beryeh (Yiddish) An efficient, competent housewife.

Birkenau Also known as Auschwitz II. One of the camps that was part of the Auschwitz complex and operated as a death camp, the sole purpose of which was killing Jews and others considered undesirable by the Nazis. Established in early 1942, the gas chambers at Birkenau used Zyklon B gas for mass murder. The camp also held four crematoria, which were constructed between March and June 1943.

British Broadcasting Corporation (BBC) The British public service broadcaster. During World War II, the BBC broadcast radio programming to Europe in German and the languages of the occupied countries. Some of this programming was used by Allied forces to send coded messages to resistance groups. It was illegal to listen to these broadcasts, but many people in Nazi-occupied Europe turned to it as the most reliable source of news.

Canaan (Hebrew) Biblical name for the Middle Eastern region that now includes Israel, the Palestinian territories, Jordan, Lebanon and parts of Syria.

catechism A reference text and guide to the Catholic religion in a question-and-answer format to help teach the doctrine of the faith.

cattle cars Freight cars used to deport Jews by rail to concentration camps and death camps. The European railways played a key logistical role in how the Nazis were able to transport millions of Jews from around Europe to killing centres in occupied Poland under the guise of "relocation." The train cars were usually ten metres long and often crammed with over a hundred people in abhorrent conditions with no water, food or sanitation. Many Jews, already weak from poor living conditions in the ghettos, died in the train cars from suffocation or illness before ever arriving at the camps.

cholent (Yiddish) A traditional Jewish slow-cooked pot stew usually eaten as the main course at the festive Shabbat lunch on Saturdays after the synagogue service and on other Jewish holidays. For Jews of Eastern European descent, the basic ingredients of *cholent* are meat, potatoes, beans and barley.

circumcision Removal of the foreskin of the penis. In Judaism, ritual circumcision is performed on the eighth day of a male infant's life in a religious ceremony known as a *brit milah* (Hebrew) or *bris* (Yiddish) to welcome him into the covenant between God and the People of Israel.

csendőr (Hungarian) The gendarmes of the pro-Hitler Arrow Cross Party. During World War II they often worked with the Gestapo in rounding up Jews, Roma and political opponents.

defect, defector To leave or abandon one's country or political party to form an allegiance with another. It was often used to describe Soviet or Soviet bloc citizens who found ways to leave the USSR or Soviet bloc countries to live in the West.

"Deutschland über Alles" (German; literally: "Germany above everything") Also known as the *Deutschlandlied* (Song of Germany), the 1848 poem was the national anthem for Germany from 1922 until 1945.

DPs (displaced persons) People who find themselves homeless and stateless at the end of a war. Following World War II, millions of people, especially European Jews, found that they had no homes to return to or that it was unsafe to do so. *See also* DP camps.

DP camps Facilities set up by the Allied authorities and the United Nations Relief and Rehabilitation Administration (UNRRA) in October 1945 to resolve the staggering refugee crisis that arose at the end of World War II. The camps provided temporary shelter and assistance to the millions of people – not only Jews – who had been displaced from their home countries as a result of the war and helped them prepare for resettlement. *See also* United Nations Relief and Rehabilitation Administration (UNRRA).

Eretz Yisrael (Hebrew) The biblical Land of Israel

Exodus The second of the five books of the Hebrew Bible, or Torah (also known as the Pentateuch). The book relates how Moses took the people of Israel out of slavery in Egypt and led them through the desert to bring them to the Promised Land, Canaan. In the desert, at Mount Sinai, God gives them the Ten Commandments (the laws to live by) and enters into a covenant with them.

forced labour battalion Unpaid labour, often under brutal conditions, that the Nazis forced millions of Jews and non-Jews to perform. In some cases, Jewish men and women were taken out of the ghettos each day and returned at night; in other cases they were transported to forced labour camps in other regions or countries.

Frank, Anne (1929–1945) A German-Jewish teenager who spent twenty-five months in hiding with her family in Amsterdam during World War II, where she wrote her famous diary, *The Diary of Anne Frank*. Anne and her family were found and arrested on August 4, 1944, and transported to Auschwitz. She died at Bergen-Belsen from typhus seven months later. Her diary has been translated into more than sixty-five languages and is taught in thousands of schools across the world.

Franz Joseph I (1830–1916) Emperor of Austria (1848–1916) and king of Hungary (1867–1916). The murder of his heir apparent, Francis Ferdinand, in Sarajevo in 1914 provided the impetus for Austria-Hungary and Germany to declare war on Serbia and precipitated the beginning of World War I.

Gestapo (German) Short for Geheime Staatspolizei, the Secret State Police of Nazi Germany. The Gestapo was the brutal force that dealt with the perceived enemies of the Nazi regime and were responsible for rounding up European Jews for deportation to the death camps. They operated with very few legal constraints and were also responsible for issuing exit visas to the residents of German-occupied areas. A number of Gestapo members also joined the Einsatzgruppen, the mobile killing squads responsible for the roundup and murder of Jews in eastern Poland and the USSR through mass shooting operations.

ghetto A confined residential area for Jews. The term originated in Venice, Italy in 1516 with a law requiring all Jews to live on a segregated, gated island known as Ghetto Nuovo. Throughout the Middle Ages in Europe, Jews were often forcibly confined to gated Jewish neighbourhoods. During the Holocaust, the Nazis forced Jews to live in crowded and unsanitary conditions in rundown districts of cities and towns. The ghetto in Levice, Hungary, where Eva Marx's grandparents were sent when they were deported from Vráble, was established in May 1944 and held more than one thousand Jews who were deported to Auschwitz one month later.

gimnázium (Hungarian; in German, *Gymnasium*) A word used throughout Central and Eastern Europe to mean high school.

Hapsburgs The royal family who headed the Austrian Empire and its successors, including the Austro-Hungarian Empire, for six centuries from the 1282 to 1918.

Hashomer Hatzair (Hebrew) The Youth Guard. A left-wing Zionist youth movement founded in Central Europe in the early twentieth century to prepare young Jews to become workers and farmers, to establish kibbutzim – collective settlements – in pre-state

Israel and work the land as pioneers. Before World War II, there were 70,000 Hashomer Hatzair members worldwide and many of those in Nazi-occupied territories led resistance activities in the ghettos and concentration camps or joined partisan groups in the forests of east-central Europe. It is the oldest Zionist youth movement still in existence. *See also* Zionism.

heymish (Yiddish; also haymishe; literally, homey) Cozy or unpretentious.

High Holidays (also High Holy Days) The autumn holidays that mark the beginning of the Jewish year and that include Rosh Hashanah (New Year) and Yom Kippur (Day of Atonement). Rosh Hashanah is observed by synagogue services where the leader of the service blows the shofar (horn), and festive meals where sweet foods, such as apples and honey, are eaten to symbolize and celebrate a sweet new year. Yom Kippur, a day of fasting and prayer at synagogue, follows ten days later.

Hlinka guard The paramilitary wing of the autonomous Slovak regime, established in October 1938. *See also* Hlinka's Slovak People's Party.

Hlinka's Slovak People's Party (HSSP) Named for its founder and first chairman, Father Andrej Hlinka, the HSSP was a strongly nationalist, Catholic, totalitarian party that became the first government of the newly autonomous Slovak Republic in 1939. Its wartime president, who had taken over as chairman of the HSSP after Hlinka's death in 1938, was Catholic priest Jozef Tiso. The Hlinka Guard, the paramilitary wing of the new autonomous Slovak regime, was established in October 1938.

Jewish houses (Budapest) Also known as "yellow star" buildings (*sárga csillagos házak*). In June 1944, three months after Germany occupied Hungary, the Nazis ordered the Jews in Budapest to move into designated buildings marked with a yellow Star of David. More than 200,000 Jews were assigned to less than two thousand apartments. They were allowed to leave the buildings for two hours in the afternoon, but only if they wore an identifying yellow Star of David on their clothing. This meant they could be easily located when the time came for them to be deported. *See also* ghetto; Star of David.

Jewish Immigrant Aid Society (JIAS) An organization that has provided a variety of services to Jewish immigrants to Canada from 1919 to the present. Its origins trace back to the first assembly of the Canadian Jewish Congress in 1919 when it was faced with a Jewish refugee crisis in Canada after World War I. In 1955 the organization changed its name to Jewish Immigrant Aid Services of Canada.

King George VI (1895–1952) Albert Frederick Arthur George was king of the United Kingdom and the British Commonwealth countries (including Canada) from 1936 until his death in 1952. He remained in London throughout the war despite the constant threat from German bombing raids. By being willing to incur the same dangers as other Londoners, refusing to flee to safety, King George became an important symbol of wartime resistance for the British people. George's eldest daughter, Queen Elizabeth II, is the current reigning monarch of England.

kosher (Hebrew) Fit to eat according to Jewish dietary laws. Observant Jews follow a system of rules known as *kashruth* that regulates what can be eaten, how food is prepared and how meat and poultry are slaughtered. Food is kosher when it has been deemed fit for consumption according to this system of rules. There are several foods that are forbidden, most notably pork products and shellfish.

Lenin, Vladimir (1870–1924) The founder of the Russian Communist Party and leader of the Bolsheviks throughout the October Revolution in 1917 and Russian Civil War (1917–1923). Lenin is considered the architect of the USSR (Union of Soviet Socialist Republics).

Lord's Prayer (in Latin, Oratio Dominica, also called Pater Noster, "Our Father") A common prayer in Christian liturgy, it appears in the New Testament in two versions (short and long) as part of the teachings of Jesus and as a model of prayer.

Marx, Karl (1818–1883) The German philosopher, historian, sociologist and theorist who inspired the revolutionary communist ideology known as Marxism. His view of history, called "historical materialism," argued that capitalist modes of production that exploited workers would ultimately lead to a class struggle and a breakdown of the economy, laying the ground for communism. According to Marx's vision, a communist society would be classless and stateless, based on a common ownership of the means of production, free access to the material goods that people need for wellbeing, and an end to wage labour and private property. Two of his most famous books are *The Communist Manifesto* (1848) and *Capital* (1867–1894).

Masaryk, Jan (1886–1948) A liberal-democratic politician who was the son of Tomáš G. Masaryk, the founder and first president of Czechoslovakia. He served as foreign minister to the Czech government-in-exile during World War II, a position he retained in the provisional, multi-party National Front government established in Czechoslovakia after its liberation from the Germans in 1945. In 1948, following the consolidation of a Communist, Soviet-led government, Jan Masaryk was found dead in his pyjamas in the courtyard of his apartment building. There was ongoing debate and investigations into whether he committed suicide, as was proclaimed by the Communist government, or whether he was thrown to his death by Communist thugs. A final investigation, concluded in December 2003, proved that Masaryk was murdered through the testimony of an expert witness who studied the position of the body when it was found. This new evidence, however, did not lead to any prosecutions.

matzah (Hebrew; also matza, matzoh, matsah; in Yiddish, matze) Crisp flatbread made of plain white flour and water that is not allowed to rise before or during baking. Matzah is the substitute for bread during the Jewish holiday of Passover, when eating bread and leavened products is forbidden.

Napoleon Bonaparte I (1769–1821) Emperor of France from 1804–1815. Considered one of the greatest military strategists in history and a promoter of liberal reform in France, known as the Napoleonic Code.

Orthodox Judaism The set of beliefs and practices of Jews for whom the observance of Jewish law is closely connected to faith; it is characterized by strict religious observance of Jewish dietary laws, restrictions on work on the Sabbath and holidays, and a modest code of dress.

patron saints Apostles, martyrs or exceptionally holy individuals who are chosen as guardians over certain areas that could include countries, churches or even professions or illnesses. In prayer, worshippers will often ask their patron saint to intercede on their behalf in heaven.

Rákosi, Mátyás (1892–1971) The Hungarian dictator who led the country as General Secretary of the Hungarian Communist Party from 1945 to 1956.

rosary (from Latin *rosium*; literally, rose garden) A set of prayers and meditations in Roman Catholic practice. The sequence includes sets of ten Hail Mary prayers preceded by one Our Father prayer and followed by a Glory Be prayer, repeated five times. To keep count, people use a string of 55 beads called rosary beads.

Sabbath/ Shabbat (Hebrew; in Yiddish, Shabbes, Shabbos) The weekly day of rest beginning Friday at sunset and ending Saturday at sundown, ushered in by the lighting of candles on Friday night and the recitation of blessings over wine and challah (egg bread); a day of celebration as well as prayer, it is customary to eat three festive meals, attend synagogue services and refrain from doing any work or travelling.

Saint Francis of Assisi (Giovanni Francesco di Bernardone; 1181/ 1182–1226) The Italian religious leader who founded the order known as the Franciscans. One of the most venerated of the Christian Saints.

Saint Nicholas Born into a wealthy family in the third century in Turkey (then Greece) Nicholas gave all his money to help the poor and the sick. December 6, Saint Nicholas Day, is a festival for children in many countries in Europe, and legends of Saint Nicholas's gift giving are the basis for Santa Claus and Father Christmas in Britain. In Hungary and Romania children leave their shoes at the window on the eve of December 5 to be filled with candies if they have been good.

Saint Theresa of Avila (1515–1582) A Carmelite nun in Spain and one of the main saints of the Roman Catholic Church. Known as a mystic.

Siege of Budapest The battle from December 24, 1944, to February 13, 1945, between German and pro-German Hungarian troops and the Soviet Red Army and Romanian army; the latter encircled Budapest to liberate the city. The Hungarian and German army surrendered on February 13, but not before the Arrow Cross had rounded up Budapest's remaining Jews into a small ghetto. The Germans, with the help of the Arrow Cross, ordered 70,000 Jews to march by foot to Austria where they were then sent to various concentration camps. Thousands were shot or died of starvation and exposure on the way. Twenty thousand more Jews were taken from the ghetto and shot along the banks of the Danube River.

SS Abbreviation for Schutzstaffel (Defence Corps). The SS was established in 1925 as Adolf Hitler's elite corps of personal bodyguards. Under the direction of Heinrich Himmler, its membership grew from 280 in 1929 to 50,000 when the Nazis came to power in 1933, and to nearly a quarter of a million on the eve of World War II. The SS was comprised of the Allgemeine-SS (General SS) and the Waffen-SS (Armed, or Combat SS). The General SS dealt with policing and the enforcement of Nazi racial policies in Germany and the Nazi-occupied countries. An important unit within the SS was the Reichssicherheitshauptamt (RSHA, the Central Office of Reich Security), whose responsibility included the Gestapo

(Geheime Staatspolizei). The SS ran the concentration and death camps, with all their associated economic enterprises, and also fielded its own Waffen-SS military divisions, including some recruited from the occupied countries. *See also* Gestapo.

Stalin, Joseph (1879–1953) The leader of the Soviet Union from 1924 until his death in 1953. Born Joseph Vissarionovich Dzhugashvili, he changed his name to Stalin (literally: man of steel) in 1903. He was a staunch supporter of Lenin, taking control of the Communist Party upon Lenin's death. Very soon after acquiring leadership of the Communist Party, Stalin ousted rivals, killed opponents in purges, and effectively established himself as a dictator. After World War II he set up Communist governments controlled by Moscow in many Eastern European states bordering and close to the USSR.

Star of David (in Hebrew, *Magen David*) The six-pointed star that is the ancient and most recognizable symbol of Judaism. During World War II, Jews in Nazi-occupied areas were frequently forced to wear a badge or armband with the Star of David on it as an identifying mark of their lesser status and to single them out as targets for persecution.

Sudeten Deutsche The approximately three million ethnic Germans (*Volksdeutsche*) living in the western border regions of Czechoslovakia before World War II. *See also* Sudetenland.

Sudetenland The western border region of former Czechoslovakia that was inhabited primarily by ethnic Germans before World War II. In an attempt to prevent the outbreak of war, Britain, France and Italy agreed to the annexation of the Sudetenland by the Third Reich as part of the Munich Agreement, which was signed on September 30, 1938.

Tiso, Father Jozef (1887–1947) A pro-Nazi Slovak cleric who became head of the fascist Slovak State from 1939 to 1945. *See also* Hlinka's Slovak People's Party (HSSP).

Szálasi, Ferenc (1897–1946) The founder and leader of the Hungarian fascist Arrow Cross Party that actively collaborated with the Nazis in Hungary, notably in the persecution and deportation of Jews.

He was convicted of war crimes and executed in 1946. *See also* Arrow Cross Party.

treif Food that is not allowed under Jewish dietary laws. *See also* kosher.

Ursuline Mother-House. The term used for Ursuline convents.

Ursuline nuns Catholic religious order founded in Italy in 1535 that is dedicated to the education of girls.

Wallenberg, Raoul (1912–1947) The Swedish humanitarian who was sent to Hungary in June 1944 by the US Refugee Board and succeeded in saving tens of thousands of Budapest Jews by issuing them Swedish certificates of protection. The Swedish government also authorized Wallenberg to set up thirty "safe houses" and organize food distribution, medical assistance and child care. Of the slightly more than 100,000 Jews that remained alive in Budapest at the end of the war, a majority were saved through his efforts.

Western Wall (also Wailing Wall; in Hebrew, *Kotel*; literally, wall) A remnant of a wall from the second Jewish Temple built by Herod the Great in Jerusalem, constructed in 19 BCE. It is considered the most sacred site in Judaism.

yellow star buildings. *See* Jewish houses (Budapest).

Yiddish A language derived from Middle High German with elements of Hebrew, Aramaic, Romance and Slavic languages, and written in Hebrew characters. Spoken by Jews in east-central Europe for roughly a thousand years from the tenth century to the mid-twentieth century, it was still the most common language among European Jews until the outbreak of World War II. There are similarities between Yiddish and contemporary German.

zeide (Yiddish; also zaide, zeyde) Grandfather.

Zionism A movement promoted by the Viennese Jewish journalist Theodor Herzl, who argued in his 1896 book *Der Judenstaat* (The Jewish State) that the best way to resolve the problem of antisemitism and persecution of Jews in Europe was to create an independent Jewish state in the historic Jewish homeland of Biblical Israel. Zionists also promoted the revival of Hebrew as a Jewish national language.

Photographs

Judy Abrams

The family of Judy Abrams' mother, Renée Kaba Grünfeld, in Savanyukut, Hungary, 1921. From left to right: Judy's grandfather, Imre Kaba; her grandmother, Anni Deutsch Kaba; her mother; her aunts Márta and Marika; her uncle Józsi; and her aunt Éva.

Renée Grünfeld. Budapest, 1940.

Judy Grünfeld Abrams at three years old. Budapest, 1940.

Judy at five years old. Budapest, 1942.

1

2

3

4

Judy (centre) sitting beside Mária Babar (second from the right), who helped her hide at the Ursuline convent in Pincehely, Hungary in 1944.

Judy, standing second from the right, with Mária and other girls at the convent in Pincehely, 1944.

Judy and the Mother Superior of the convent. Pincehely, 1944.

Judy (right) with Mária, now Mária Babar-Kennedy, on the day that Mária was honoured as a Righteous Among the Nations by Yad Vashem, the Holocaust Martyrs' and Heroes' Remembrance Authority. California, 1994.

1

2

1   Renée Grünfeld, Judy's mother, after the war. Budapest, 1947.
2   Judy at eleven years old. Budapest, 1948.

Judy at twelve years old on the SS *Scythia* on her way to Canada, 1949.

1 The SS *Scythia*, the ship that took Judy and her parents from Bremen, Germany to Halifax, Nova Scotia, 1949.

2 Judy, centre, with her parents, Renée and László Grünfeld, at their first apartment on Ridgevale Avenue (now called St. Kevin Avenue). Montreal, 1949.

3 Judy in her school uniform. Montreal, 1950.

4 Judy wearing her first pair of slacks. Montreal, circa 1951.

Judy Abrams at the Jewish General Hospital Annual Gala fundraiser. Montreal, 1959.

1 Mária Babar-Kennedy (left) with Judy's aunt Marika (centre), Judy's father, László Grünfeld (right) and Judy's younger son, Eugene. Montreal, circa 1966.

2 Judy with her husband, older son and daughter-in-law in New York City, 2010. From left to right: Judy's husband, Tevia Abrams; Judy; their son Ira Abrams and his wife, Rachel Krucoff.

3 Judy's younger son, Eugene Abrams (right), his son, Émile, (centre) and his wife, Julie LaVergne, in their house in Longueuil, 2010.

Judy and Tevia at Iguassu Falls on the border between Brazil and Argentina in 2009.

Eva Felsenburg Marx

1 Eva Felsenburg Marx's paternal grandfather, Heinrich Felsenburg.
2 Her maternal great-grandparents, Ignacz and Rosa Berceller Rosenbaum.
3 Her maternal grandfather, Gabriel (Gabor) Weisz.
4 Her maternal grandmother, Sari Rosenbaum Weisz.

The prayer book that saved Gabor Weisz's life when he was shot during World War I.

1   Eva's father, Eugene (Jenö) Felsenburg, standing on the far right, when he served in the Austro-Hungarian army during World War I. 1918.

2   Her mother, Helen (Ilonka) Weisz, left, with her younger sister, Hedi, circa 1916.

3   Eva's parents, Helen and Eugene Felsenburg, in 1929.

1 Eva's hometown of Brno, with a view of the Spielberg Castle in the background. The photo was taken in 1987.

2 The department store Dom Moderné Brněnký (D M B) – "The House of the Modern Brnoesse" – where Eva's parents had their fur boutique before World War II. Brno, 1987.

3 Eva's grandparents' house in Vráble, Slovakia. The photo was taken in 1987.

1

2

3

1 This postcard, sent to Eva in 1980 from her devoted caregiver Marka Piesikova, shows what Vráble's main street looked like before World War II.

2 Eva at about two years old, soon after her arrival in Vráble, with her aunt Hedi (left), her mother (centre) and her grandmother, Sari Weisz, 1939.

3 Marka Piesikova in 1944.

1

2

3

1 Eva's maternal relatives in Paks, 1940. Second from the left is her second cousin, Willie Rosenbaum; third from the left is her mother; Eva is standing in the centre beside her grandmother, Sari Weisz; and third from the right is Eva's great-uncle Matyi.

2 Eva at about five years old in Vráble, 1942.

3 Eva (centre) with her friends in Vráble, circa 1942.

1 Eva (third from right) at a Purim party after the war. Brno, 1947.

2 Eva, far right, at ten years old with her friends Karl Hanak (left), Rudy Hanak (second from the left) and Jiří Kadlec. Koněšín, Czechoslovakia, 1948.

3 Eva and her friend Jiří in Brno, 1948.

4 Eva at age eleven in Brno, 1949.

1   Eva (left), with her aunt Hedvig (centre), her father's eldest sister, and her mother (right) on Mount Royal. It was Aunt Hedvig who sponsored the Felsenburg family's immigration to Canada. Montreal, 1949.

2   Eva at nineteen years old with her mother at Eva's graduation from MacDonald College. Ste. Anne de Bellevue, 1956.

3   Helen Felsenburg's ninety-fifth birthday. Montreal, 2003.

1

2   3

Eva's family at her daughter Sarah's wedding. Left to right: (back row) Eva's husband, Herbert Marx, and son-in-law, Andrew Shalit; (middle row) Sarah Marx; Eva's son, Robert; Robert's wife, Rena, and Eva; (seated in front) Eva's mother, Helen Felsenburg. 1995.

Eva's grandsons Harry, six, and David, one. 2011.

Eva's granddaughters Ella (left), nine, and Hannah (right), six. 2010.

Index

Abrams, Eugene (Judy's son), xxiii, 64

Abrams, Ira (Judy's son), xxiii, 64

Abrams, Judy (née Judit Grünfeld): in Austria, xxiii, 48–51; childhood in Budapest, 7–10, 31–37; escape from Hungary, 41–43, 46–49, 71; in hiding in Budapest; xxi, 19–21; as Ilona Papp, xiii, xxi, 8, 10, 22; immigration to Canada, xxiii, xxix, 39, 50–52, 70; in Michigan, 64–66; in Montreal, 52–61, 71; at Ursuline convent, xiii, 9–15

Abrams, Tevia (Judy's husband), xxiii, 64

Ági (Judy's childhood friend), 41, 44

Aix-en-Provence (France), 130

Aladar (Eva's uncle), 112, 134

Alfred Joyce School (Montreal), 121

Államvédelmi Osztálya (ÁVO), 43–44

Allies, 103

American-occupied zone, xxiii, 48–49

Anschluss, xxv

Aranka (in Nitra), 102–104

Army PX (Post Exchange), 50

Arrow Cross (Nyilas), xvi, xx–xxi, xxii, 16, 21–22, 25–26

"Auntie Superintendent" (Budapest), 20–23

Auschwitz, xxi, xxvii, 16, 34, 98, 107, 108, 118, 133

Austria, xx, xxv, 48–49

Austro-Hungarian Empire, xix, xxiv, 84, 85, 143

ÁVO. See Államvédelmi Osztálya.

Babar, Mária, xxi, xxii, 9, 15–17, 19–20, 22, 27–28, 31, 36–37, 70

Banska Bystrica (Slovakia), 134

Barrington, Miss (Montreal High School for Girls), 127

Beneš, Edvard, xxviii, 118

Beneš Technical College (Brno), 84

Bergen-Belsen, xxii, 15, 16, 70

Berlin (Germany), 85

Bohemia, xxiv–xxv, xxvi, xxvii, 83, 91

Bratislava (Slovakia), 93
Bremen (Germany), 50, 53
British Broadcasting Corporation
   (BBC), 103
Brno (Czechoslovakia), xxiv, xxvi,
   xxviii, 83, 84, 91–92, 109–113, 117,
   127–128
Brno Mountain, 84, 111
Brown, Miss (Iona Avenue School),
   56–58
Budapest (Hungary), xiii, xviii,
   xxi–xxii, xxvii, xxviii, 15–16, 19,
   21, 41, 43, 86–87, 92, 96–97, 112,
   133, 135
Bumbalek, Mr. and Mrs., 85
Canada, 57, 118–119
Čechova, Helena, 110–111
Chaplin, Charlie, 120
communism, xxi, xxviii, 42–43, 49,
   72, 118, 149
convent. See Ursuline convent.
csendőr (gendarmes), 11, 141
Cuci (Aranka's son), 102
Czechoslovak Republic, xxiv–xxvi.
   See also Czechoslovakia.
Czechoslovakia, xv, xix, xx, xxv–
   xxvi, xxviii, 83–85, 88–89, 91, 92,
   110, 111, 117–118, 120, 139
Danube River (Hungary), xxii,
   21–22, 26, 57, 96, 138
de Havilland, Olivia, 120
Desző (Judy's uncle), 33
Deutsch, Hedvig (Eva's aunt), 118,
   120, 133, 135
Deutsch, Tibi (Eva's cousin), 135
Dickens, Charles, 87

DP (displaced persons) camp, xxiii,
   50
Drobna, Milada, 111
Edith (Eva's cousin), 133
Eichmann, Adolf, xx
Elmgrove Elementary School
   (Montreal), xxix
Erika (Eva's cousin), 112
Escobar summer camp, 60–61
Erzsi (Judy's maid), 44
Éva (Judy's camp friend), 44
Fatelessness (Imre Kertész), 135
Feldstein, Marilyn, 122, 128
Felsenburg, Eugene ("Jenö," Eva's
   father), xvii, xxvi, xxvii–xxix, 83,
   84–89, 91–92, 98–99, 102–103,
   104, 107–109, 113, 118–119,
   122–123, 125–127, 129–130, 136
Felsenburg, Eva. See Marx, Eva (née
   Felsenburg).
Felsenburg, Eva (Eva's cousin), 99,
   108–109, 114–115, 134
Felsenburg, Helen ("Ilonka" née
   Weisz, Eva's mother), xvii,
   xxv, xxvi, xxvi, xxix, 83, 84–89,
   99–100, 102, 107, 109–110, 113,
   115, 119, 122–123, 125, 127–133, 136
Felsenburg, Heinrich (Eva's paternal
   grandfather), 88, 112
Felsenburg, Herta, 99
Felsenburg, Morris (Eva's paternal
   great-uncle), 85
Felsenburg, Nandor (Eva's cousin),
   99, 108–109, 134
Felsenburg, Norbert (Eva's uncle),
   133

Felsenburg, Pauli (Eva's cousin), 133
Felsenburg, Erno (Eva's uncle), 133
Felsenburg, Ilka (Eva's aunt), 133
"Final Solution," xx, 22
Frank, Anne, 16
Gabler Hotel (Vienna), 49
George (Judy's camp boyfriend),
    44–45, 59
German soldiers, 16, 92, 98, 105
Germany, xv, xviii, xx, xxiv–xxvi,
    xxvii, 7–8, 9, 21, 29, 84, 88–89,
    91, 92, 101, 104–106
Gestapo, 101. See also Nazis.
Géza (Judy's uncle), 33
Golden Age Association
    (Montreal), 130
Gömbös, Gyula, xix
Grünfeld, Elza (Judy's aunt), 32–33,
    35, 36
Grünfeld, Helen (Ilonka, Judy's
    aunt), 34
Grünfeld, Judit. See Abrams, Judy
    (née Grünfeld).
Grünfeld, Katrin (Judy's maternal
    grandmother), 34, 42
Grünfeld, László (Judy's father),
    xviii, xxii, xxiii, 8, 15, 35, 37,
    42–44, 49–50, 55, 63–67
Grünfeld, Lula (Judy's aunt), 35
Grünfeld, Max (Judy's uncle), 34, 35
Grünfeld, Renée (née Kaba, Judy's
    mother), xvii, xxii, xxiii, 8, 15,
    32, 35–37, 39–40, 42–44, 47–49,
    51–52, 64–67, 69–71, 73
Gulliver, Mr. (principal of Iona
    Avenue School), 55–56

Gyuri, (Judy's music teacher), 42, 44
Halifax (Canada), 52
Hanak family, 113–115
Hanak, Karl, 113–115
Hanak, Rudy, 113–115
Hapsburg Empire. See Austro-
    Hungarian Empire.
Hashomer Hatzair, xxviii, 109. See
    also Zionism.
Heine, Heinrich, 66
Herman, Livora, 94
Hilda (Judy's aunt), 33
Hitler, Adolf, xv, xix, xxv, 16, 83, 84,
    89, 91
Hlinka Guard, xxvi, 91
Hlinka's Slovak People's Party
    (HSSP), xxvii, 91
Holocaust Museum (Vilnius), 72
Holtzman family (landlords in
    Montreal), 120–121, 128
Holtzman, Maisie, 121, 122
Horthy, Miklós, xix
Hungary, xviii–xxi, xxv, xxvi, xxvii,
    7–8, 9, 16, 42–43, 56–57, 63, 64,
    71, 85, 91
India, xxiii
Iona Avenue School (Montreal),
    55–58
Iren (née Felsenburg, Eva's aunt),
    134
Israel, xxviii, 111, 118–119, 130
Janovic, Mr., 125
Jewish Code, xxvii
Jewish "yellow star" houses
    (Budapest), xxii, 16, 144
Jewish Immigrant Aid Society

(JIAS), 120

Jozef, Emperor Franz I, 93

Judka (in Nitra), 102

Kaba, Anni ("Nagyi," Judy's grandmother), xxi, xxii, 16–17, 19–21,
22–23, 26–28, 31–32, 41

Kaba, Imre (Judy's grandfather),
xxv, 34, 35

Kaba, Marika (Judy's aunt), xxi,
xxii, 16–17, 19–20, 22, 25, 27–28,
31–32

Kadlec, Frantisek, 85–86, 113

Kadlec, Gerti, 85–86, 113, 117

Kadlec, Jiři, 85, 114

Kállay, Miklós, xx

Kanawana (YMCA summer camp),
60

Kertész, Imre, 135

King George VI, 55

Klári (in Budapest), 40–42, 44

Komarek family, 118

Koněšín (Bohemia), 113, 114–115

Kovacs, Blanka (Eva's aunt), 134

Kovacs, Erzsi (Eva's cousin), 134

Kovacs, Joska (Eva's uncle), 134

Lake Balaton (Hungary), 10, 42, 44

Lalli (Eva's cousin), 112

Langmour, Mrs. (Alfred Joyce
School), 122

Laurentian Mountains (Quebec), 60

Le Havre (France), 119

Lenin, Vladimir, 47

Levice (Slovakia), 98

Lithuania, 69, 73

MacDonald College (Montreal),
xxiii, xxix, 128–129, 130

Mari (Judy's friend at the convent),
13

Marta (née Felsenburg, Eva's aunt),
134

Martineau, Miss, 126

Marx, Ella (Eva's granddaughter),
xxix, 136

Marx, Eva (née Felsenburg): in
Brno, 85–86, 107–119; immigration to Canada, xvii, xxiv, 110,
118–123; in Montreal, 125–132; in
Nitra, xxvii, 101–106; in Vráble,
xiii, xxvi–xxvii, 91–98, 107–108

Marx, Hannah (Eva's granddaughter), xxix, 136

Marx, Herbert (Eva's husband),
xxix, 129, 132

Marx, Karl, 47

Marx, Robert (Eva's son), xxix,
130–131, 132

Marx, Sarah (Eva's daughter), xxix,
132

Masaryk, Jan, 118

Masaryk, Tomáš Garrigue, xxiv,
xxv, 118

Masaryk University (Brno), 84

Mátra Mountains (Hungary), 10, 42

McKenzie, Mrs. (Alfred Joyce
School), 122

Mendel, Gregor, 84

Michigan (USA), xxiii, 64

Michigan State University, xxiii

Minsk (Belarus), xxvi

Monika (friend in Vienna), 49

Montreal (Canada), xxiii, 39, 63–64,
67, 69, 73, 84, 120

Montreal High School for Girls, xxiii, 127

Moravia, xxiv–xxv, xxvi, xxvii, 83, 91

Mother Superior, Ursuline convent, 10–11, 15. See also Ursuline convent.

Mount Zobor, 104

Mudrakova, Kaja (Eva's friend in Brno), 111

munkaszolgálat, 16, 33

Museum of Genocide Victims (Vilnius), 72

N., Mr. and Mrs. (from Bucharest), 50–53

Nagyi (Judy's grandmother). See Kaba, Anni ("Nagyi," Judy's grandmother).

Napoleon Bonaparte, 84

Nazis, xv, xxi, 91. See also Gestapo.

Nitra (Slovakia), xiii, xvii, xxvii, xxviii, 93, 98–99, 101, 104–105, 107–109

Numerous Clausus Act, xix

Nuremberg Laws, xv

Nyilas. See Arrow Cross.

Orthodox Judaism, 93, 113

Paks (Hungary), 96

Palestine, 135. See also Israel.

Papp, Ilona (Judy's false identity), xiii, xxi, 8, 10, 22. See also Abrams, Judy.

Paul (Judy's uncle), 34

Pavlov (Bohemia), 113–114

Peter (Judy's cousin), 33–34

Petőfi, 57

Pier 21 (Halifax), xxiii

Piesik, Dusan, 133

Piesikova, Marka (Eva's maid), xvi, xxvi, 86, 91–92, 93–94, 108, 109–110, 133

Pincehely (Hungary), 13–15, 16. See also Ursuline convent.

Pityu (Eva's cousin), 112

Poland, xv, xx

Prague (Czechoslovakia), xxvi

PX. See Army PX (Post Exchange).

Québec City (Canada), 119–120

Rafman, Dr., 87

Rákosi, Mátyás, 47

Rientova, Eva (Eva's friend in Brno), 111

Righteous Among the Nations, xxi

Rita (Judy's neighbour in Montreal), 58–60

Rise and Fall of the Third Reich, The (William L. Shirer), 136

Roger (Judy' camp friend), 60–61

Ronn, Joshua (Rosenbaum, Eva's cousin), 97, 135

Rosenbaum, Chaim, 135

Rosenbaum, Ignacz (Eva's maternal great-grandfather), 96–97

Rosenbaum, Lilly, 135

Rosenbaum, Naomi, 135

Rosenbaum, Rosa (née Berceller, Eva's maternal great-grandmother), 96–97

Rosenbaum, Willie (Eva's uncle), 97, 135

Rosenbaum, Willy (Eva's mother's cousin), 119, 135

Rosenbaum, Wilma (Eva's aunt), 135
Rosh Hashanah, 112
Roter Krebs Hotel (Vienna), 49
Sagher, Peter, 111–112
St. Francis of Assisi, 14
St. Theresa of Avila, 14
Salzburg (Austria), 48, 49–50, 55
Samson, Mr. (Alfred Joyce School), 121
Second Republic of Czechoslovakia, xxviii
Seltzer, Peter (Eva's cousin), 84, 113, 134
Seltzer, Pista (Eva's cousin), 84, 113, 134
Seltzer, Sida (Eva's father's cousin), 113, 134
Shalit, David (Eva's grandson), xxix, 136
Shalit, Harry (Eva's grandson), xxix, 136
Siege of Budapest, 21–23
Silesia (Slovakia), xxv
Sir George Williams College (Montreal), xxiii, xxix
Slovakia, xv, xxi, xxiv–xxv, xxvi, xxvii, 83, 85, 91, 101, 104
Slovak Jewish Council, xxi
Sobibor, xxvii
Soviet Red Army, xxvii, 19, 21, 27, 36, 49, 104, 106
Soviet Union, xx, xxii, 31, 118
Spielberg Castle (Brno), xxvi, 84
Spielberg Mountain. See Brno Mountain.
SS Samaria, 119

SS Scythia, 50, 52
Stalin, Joseph, 47
Star of David, xx–xxi, 8, 11, 13, 16, 92
State of Israel. See Israel.
Ste. Anne de Bellevue (Quebec), xxix, 128
Strathcona Academy (Montreal), 122
Subcarpathian Ruthenia, xxv, xxvi
Sudetenland, xxv, 88, 149
Sudeten Deutsch, 84
Sweden, xxii, 39, 40
Switzerland, xxii
Szálasi, Ferenc, xx, 16
Tamaci néni (in Nitra), 99
Terezin (Theresienstadt), xxvi
Tiso, Father Jozef, xxvi, xxvii, 91. See also Hlinka's Slovak People's Party.
Tomi (Judy's cousin), 33–34
Topoľčany (Slovakia), 83
United Nations Population Fund, xxiii
Ursuline convent, xvi, xxi, 9–15
Veronika (Judy's friend in Montreal), 56
Vienna (Austria), 43, 48–49, 55, 58, 64, 84, 104
Vilnius (Lithuania), 72
Vladar, Mr. (in Montreal), 120
Volksdeutsche, xxv. See also Sudeten Deutsch.
Vráble (Slovakia), xiii, xvi, xxvi–xxvii, xxviii, 83, 86–87, 91–93, 95–98, 107–108
Vrba, Rudolf, xxi

Vrba-Wetzler report, xxi, xxii
Wallenberg, Raoul, xxii, 133, 150
Weisz, Gabriel ("Gabor," Eva's maternal grandfather), xxvi–xxvii,
    87, 91, 93, 107
Weisz, Hedi (Eva's aunt) 88, 94, 107
Weisz, Juditka (Eva's cousin), 107
Weisz, Matyi (Eva's mother's uncle),
    86, 135
Weisz, Miriam (Eva's mother's
    aunt), 86, 97, 112, 134–35
Weisz, Sari (née Rosenbaum, Eva's
    grandmother), xxvi–xxvii, 91,
    93–96, 97, 107
West Hill High School (Montreal),
    xxiii
Western Wall (Israel), 130, 150
Wetzler, Alfred, xxi
World War I, 85, 88, 93
Yad Vashem, xxi
yellow star. See Star of David.
yellow star houses. See Jewish "yellow star" houses (Budapest).
Yom Kippur, 112
Zionism, xxviii. 8–9, 37. See also
    Hashomer Hatzair.
Žitava River (Vráble), 94
Zobor monastery, 105–106
Zsuzsa (Judy's cousin), 22, 37

The Azrieli Foundation was established in 1989 to realize and extend the philanthropic vision of David J. Azrieli, C.M., C.Q., M.Arch. The Foundation's mission is to support a wide spectrum of initiatives in education and research. The Azrieli Foundation is an active supporter of programs in the fields of Jewish education, the education of architects, scientific and medical research, and education in the arts. The Azrieli Foundation's many well-known initiatives include: the Holocaust Survivor Memoirs Program, which collects, preserves, publishes and distributes the written memoirs of survivors in Canada; the Azrieli Institute for Educational Empowerment, an innovative program successfully working to keep at-risk youth in school; and the Azrieli Fellows Program, which promotes academic excellence and leadership on the graduate level at Israeli universities.